Table of Contents

Introduction	A personal note	7
one	The Integrity of the Word of God	13
two	Know Your Enemy, Satan	22
three	Know Your Father, God	37
four	Job's Problems	63
five	Paul's Thorn	79
six	What is an Infirmity?	86
seven	What is an Affliction?	89
eight	Does God Test Us?	94
nine	What Does God Use to Chasten, Reprove, Teach and Perfect Us?	103
ten	What Has God Done For Us in Jesus?	110
eleven	What Can We Do Because of What Jesus Has Done?	114
twelve	What Does God Allow?	119

It might seem that I would be biased towards this book, its message, its author, being that my dad is the man behind the pen. I have lived through it's evolution from the original searches through the Strong's Concordance in my early childhood to the ensuing realizations, organization of thought and sharing with many who need to know. But beyond my history with it, beyond the attachment I have to the inflection I hear in the words, and the soft eyes and wide smile I see behind the sentiments, I believe wholeheartedly in the message itself. In the idea that there is a God, and He is good and worth trusting in.

Once you 'get' this idea into your head, it is hard not to gain frustration with the common Christian vernacular, with the well meaning sentiments about 'everything happening for a reason!' or about 'everything being under God's control' when a child dies, or a natural disaster wipes out a village, or when sickness and disease strike. Your stomach turns a bit at pretty songs that are meant to move us, that speak of God in these mysterious puppet-master sort of terms. There are so many trite ways our culture has come up with to say 'bad stuff happens and we don't understand WHY!'

The problem with those answers that point to God as the cause, or 'allower', is that they leave you hurting and angry at the very one who provides healing. They leave you questioning and untrusting what kind of 'Father' would play sick games like that and call it love. Many people either forge ahead still trying to believe that God is good, even if it is in some twisted way we mere mortals can never understand, or they decide none of it is worth believing in anyway. I hope for you reading, the words on these pages provide another way of thinking, one that you had dared to hope could maybe be true. Keep in mind that daring to believe in such things won't be a fast or slow road to popularity, people get outright angry about the idea of God *not* being the giver of Bad Things, but it is an insight worth clinging to, even if it feels, at times, a little alone 'out there'.

Growing up as a Pastor's child can be tough – you have all those "Footloose" comparisons and various expectations of 'church people' to battle against. Some PK's also have the added turmoil of parental expectations, making sure they keep up the image, or watching their parents live two different lives inside and outside of the walls of their home. I am forever and amazingly grateful that never had to be me.

I have spent my life, watching and learning incredible authenticity from both of my parents. Watching them be who they are and passionately follow a belief system worth living for. They are the real deal, both of them, full of compassion and grace and love and so much knowledge that I desperately hope will seep through the DNA we share and infuse me, in turn, with a bit of all they are.

For you, dear Reader, I am happy you are here, holding this book, these years, these struggles and thoughts and answers in your hand. My prayer is that my father's heart and words will travel through the pages and speak to your heart in a way that only God can orchestrate.

Peace,

Talitha Martin

Introduction

I finally got it. After nearly ten years of struggling with my Christian walk, I finally got it. There is real help, and real hope, and real answers for real people's real problems in the Word of God. When I finally got it, I began to realize that one of the greatest gaps in the understanding of Christian people is the very basic issue of God's character. This book is a foundational brick for that gap. This book is a simple study of a few of the most basic of the real questions people ask in their secret hearts — in the private place we all keep, where we ask of ourselves, and (if we will be honest) of God, the REALLY HARD questions.

It originally started out as a simple Bible study, done for a friend of mine, who called me one day filled with one of those REALLY HARD questions.

"John", she said, "Why would God give an innocent five year-old cancer?"

After an hour of trying to explain that God is not a child abuser, it finally dawned on me that she was completely lacking the foundation to understand the simplicity and directness of the character and nature of God. So, I determined to sketch out a few verses, with which to Biblically prove to her that God is really a lot nicer guy than most of His kids think. Six weeks later at four to six hours a day, the outline from which this book is taken, came together. I have taught that outline through some thirty-plus times in the past fifteen years, and it has never failed to help "turn on the lights" for someone. I don't say that to toot my own horn, I say that to prepare you to hear from God.

Get ready.

He's talking to you.

Please let me forewarn you: #1: This is not, nor was it ever meant to be, a complete and definitive study on the several subjects covered. #2: I am not now, nor do I have a desire to be, a Greek or Hebrew scholar. All the references made to those languages and the peculiarities of them have been gathered from my main study tools—Strong's Concordance, and a King James Bible. The only other sources I may have used will be quoted as we go.

So, why even bother to explain all this? Because I believe that a mind unsatisfied with the "pat" answers can, with a little sweat and some honest questions, arrive at the truth. And the Truth, in the final analysis, is the ONLY thing that counts. I do not think that the ideas presented here are unique. I do not think they are the truth just because I believe them. I believe they are the truth because God has presented them in His Word. For me, that's enough. It is the truth that sets you free, not my opinion of the truth. It is the truth that sets you free, not my version of the truth. It is the truth that sets you free, not some kind of doctrinal superiority. If this simple book can open up your heart and mind, so God can teach you the truth, my mission is complete.

So, lay aside your pre-set ideas, and maybe for the first time, be really unafraid to face some of your own really hard questions. In the process, trust your loving Heavenly Father to show you the real truth. My desire for you is not that you think like me, or even that you agree with me. My desire for you is that you enter into a freedom that only the truth can provide for you. If you get angry, you are not free. If you sneer, you are not free. If you feel doctrinally superior, you are a

Pharisee, and are definitely not free. If I can help you, in some small way, to fall in Love with Jesus more than you ever have, you will be free. Free to enjoy your walk with God. Free to enjoy your work. Free to enjoy your family and your life. Free to enjoy yourself, and free to enjoy your world. I believe the Scriptures support the idea that the will of your Heavenly Father is for you to be FREE.

Get Real

one
The Integrity of the Word of God

As with every other book we have ever read, there is a purpose to the sequence in which this one is laid out. That's the reason we start with a look at the integrity of the Word of God. If we do not develop an absolute and all-encompassing trust in the integrity of God's Word, not even the Almighty Himself can reach us with the answers we need. Somehow, please understand. God really is smart enough to say exactly what He means, and He really is honest enough to mean exactly what He says.

I had been born again, Spirit-filled and called to preach for a little over seven years before I finally came to grips with this one small fundamental: The Bible is a real book, with real words, and each of them has a real definition. I finally figured it out. I can learn to treat the Bible as if God actually knows what He's talking about. I can learn to give God's word at least as much respect as I have always given my earthly Dad's word. In doing those two things, I will come to a place of understanding that surpasses all that my artificial study aids have given me. When I finally came to grips with that one small fundamental, I began, for the first time to grow up in my knowledge of God.

When I treated Him and His Word the same as I did a man of integrity whom I respected, I began to find out what kind of fellow He is. I also found out that religious people had lied to me all my life. I don't believe they really meant to lie, but they lied. They told me God was angry and offended when I sinned. They told me I was such a dull, hollow-brained idiot (not in so many words, but the effect was the same) that if my Heavenly Father wanted to get my attention or teach me a lesson, He would give me car wrecks, diseases of all kinds, and maybe kill or cripple my children. I was taught that my brother died at 27, leaving a 23 year-old wife and three children under five, because God wanted to punish my mother for not being a good enough mom. I was told that when a baby died, it was because God wanted another flower in His Garden in Heaven. I was told that I lost two fingers on my right hand in a car wreck because God was trying to get my attention.

He got it. The car wreck came, I was upside down on the highway with gas running all over the place, and I wanted more than anything to hear from God whatever He wanted to teach me. I was never more focused on God in my life. Now that's a pretty good statement, because I was saved, I was Spirit-filled, I was called to preach, and I did hear from God on a regular basis. However, once I thought I understood that God had engineered that car wreck so He could get my attention, try though I would, I didn't hear one little peep from the Spirit of God for four very long, dry years. My prayer life, formerly rich and active, dried up like a raisin. The Scriptures might as well have been Greek (no pun intended) for all I could understand of what I tried to read. I was dying inside. I saw myself becoming an angry old man at thirty. Then Freddy, a friend from Bible College in Oregon, sent me six tapes by a preacher I had never heard of before.

I had never heard anything so remarkable in my life. He sounded as if God could have been a real person, with an understandable character, a knowable nature, and everything! At last! Hope!! If he can know God, as if He's a regular guy, maybe I can too! As soon as that idea soaked through the fog in my head, I heard from God!! That familiar, soft, sweet, smooth voice I had longed for in my spirit, swelled inside me, and filled me.

"I did not give you the car wreck. I saved your life."

I wept.

That was all He said, but it suddenly began to bring everything into perspective for me. I saw God's character exalted to its proper place in my life. He was no longer a guy filled with anger and bitterness and foul tempers at being thwarted, like I was. He no longer said one thing in His Word, and did something else in actual practice. To me, He just became honest, word and deed. He became not just my Savior-Who-Can-Do-Whatever-He-Wants-And-You-Never-Know-What-That-May-Be-So-You-Just-Better-Watch-It-Bucko but He became, in a moment of time, Lord. Sovereign Lord. Sovereign Lord with a Sovereign Plan for my life. Sovereign Lord with a Sovereign Expressed Will, in His Sovereign Word, which He cannot change without damage to His own integrity. Faith in the integrity of God's Word is the bedrock of all understanding of God's nature. If we can believe the Word of God, we can believe what the Word says about itself.

2 Timothy 3:16 — "All scripture is given by inspiration of God ... " The word "inspiration" comes from a compound Greek word—"theo," meaning "God," and "pneustos," meaning "breathed." All scripture is God-breathed or God-spoken.

The Bible is God-spoken. If we can learn to treat the opening of our Bible as if we were standing in the presence of Jehovah, Our Father, close enough to feel His breath, it would change the way we treat our time spent in the Word. It is far simpler to develop a love relationship with the most honest person in the universe, than it is to try to understand a "Gawd" who is "beyond understanding" as most of us have been taught.

Hebrews 4:12-13 — "For the Word of God is quick," (this Greek word means 'having or possessing life') "and powerful," (This Greek word, 'energeo,' means 'having or possessing energy') "and sharper than any two-edged sword, piercing even to the dividing asunder of soul and spirit, and of the joints and marrow, and is a discerner of the thoughts and intents of the heart. Neither is there any creature that is not manifest in his sight: but all things are naked and opened unto the eyes of him with whom we have to do." The Word possesses its own life and its own energy! So, who is "him with whom we have to do?"

Read on!

John 1:1, 14 says — "In the beginning was the Word and the Word was with God and the Word was God, and the Word was made flesh and dwelt among us ..." Him "with whom we have to do" is Jesus, the Word of God. Jesus and the Word are one!! Don't just (musical interlude) "have a little talk with Jesus, and tell Him all about our troubles!" Take it to the Word and get an answer that is filled with power and Life!!! The Word of God is able to judge human motives—all by itself! The Word has Life and Energy. For what purpose? To cause itself to bear fruit when it is planted by faith. Jesus said in Luke 8:11 that the Word of God is a seed! So plant!!!

Mark 13:31 — "Heaven and earth will pass away, but my words shall not pass away." How much more stability can we expect? God Himself said His Word was good enough to outlast the sidereal universe that supports our very existence. So, why do we still wonder if it's really true? If we absolutely have to doubt something, let us doubt our own doubts, not God's Everlasting Word.

"But Pastor John! I just have a hard time believing!!"

You what????? You what????????? Don't try to convince yourself that you have a hard time believing. We may have a hard time believing God, but our believer is not broken in any way—it's working just fine!

You have a hard time believing? Horse Feathers! We believe our own doubts! We believe our own, totally irrational fears! We believe, completely, our own negative and destructive assessment of ourselves! Why do we believe that and not the Word of God? Because we choose to do so. WE are the ones in charge of what we do, or do not, believe.

If we have determined that what we believe up to this point is not getting us any deeper into the things of God, or helping us overcome the problems of our life—we need to change!! We need to Decide to believe God!

"You make it sound soooooooo easy."

It is not easy. But then, doubt, fear and failure are surely not easy either. It is not easy, but it is simple. It takes courage to stand against our own fleshly desires and demands and make ourselves believe the Word of God and stand on it in faith. It takes tenacity in applying the simple principles of renewing our mind. We will discuss this subject in step-by-step detail a little later.

Psalm 119:89 — "Forever, O Lord, thy word is settled (the Hebrew word here means 'established') in heaven." Praise God. As far as heaven is concerned, whatever the Word says is an established fact. If God thought enough of a statement to make sure it got recorded in His Word, He thinks enough of it, as an established fact, to make sure it comes to pass in our life.

Jeremiah 1:12 — "... I will hasten my word, to perform it." God is making an unqualified promise to Jerry the Prophet that He will make sure that His Word gets done. I know this—God doesn't like Jerry the Prophet any better than He likes you and me. If God makes and keeps promises to not-especially-special Jerry, He will both make and keep His promises to not-especially-special you and me.

Read this next passage of Scripture very carefully. In it you'll find something that Jesus said was the key to successful living. He said there was only ONE thing that was needful, and it is something a person can choose to do, or not, as they decide.

Luke 10:38-42 — "Now it came to pass, as they went, that he entered into a certain village: and a certain woman named Martha received him into her house. And she had a sister called Mary, which also sat at Jesus' feet, and heard his word. But Martha was cumbered about much serving, and came to him, and said, 'Lord, dost thou not care that my sister hath left me to serve alone? Bid her therefore that she help me.' And Jesus answered and said unto her, 'Martha, Martha, thou art careful and troubled about many things: But one thing is needful: and Mary hath chosen that good part, which shall not be taken away from her.'"

Jesus said there was only one thing needful—The Word. What did Mary choose? To hear the Word. Jesus called that the "good part." If we choose the Word, and plant it like a seed in our heart, it will not, it can not, be taken away from us.

Proverbs 4:20-23 — "My son, attend to my words; incline thine ear to my sayings. Let them not depart from thine eyes; keep them in the midst of thine heart. For they are life to those that find them, and health to all their flesh. Keep thy heart with all diligence; for out of it are the issues of life."

What are His "words" and His "sayings" if not the Word of God? So, what are we supposed to do with the Word of God? Attend! Pay attention! Why is that so tough? Because the Word of God doesn't make our flesh "feel" anything. We have become so very accustomed to refusing to move until we see or feel something—until our flesh gets satisfied—that we apply that standard of motivation even to spiritual things, which have no kind of connection to our flesh at all.

When we pay attention to God's Word, where does it go? It doesn't go toward making our flesh feel or do something, but it will give us life, and it will have a beneficial effect, even on our flesh. God says that His Word will produce health to all our flesh. I just have to believe that God is smart enough to say exactly what He means and that He's honest enough to mean exactly what He says.

"What about all those good people I know who are in bad health of one kind or another? Are you saying that if they just read their Bibles, that they will get well?"

That question, and other good ones like it will be answered as we continue. Read on!!

Matthew 8:5-13 — "And when Jesus was entered into Capernaum, there came to him a centurion, beseeching him, And saying, 'Lord, my servant lieth at home sick of the palsy, and grievously tormented.' And Jesus saith unto him 'I will come and heal him.' The centurion answered and said, 'Lord, I am not worthy that thou shouldest come under my roof: but speak the word only, and my servant shall be healed. For I am a man under authority, having soldiers under me: and I say to this man 'Go,' and he goeth; and to another, 'Come,' and he cometh; and to my servant, 'Do this,' and he doeth it.' And when Jesus heard it, he marveled, and said to them that followed, 'Verily I say unto you, I have not found so great faith, no, not in Israel. And I say unto you, that many shall come from the east and west, and shall sit down with Abraham, and Isaac and Jacob, in the Kingdom of Heaven. But the children of the kingdom shall be cast out into outer darkness: There shall be weeping and gnashing of teeth.' And Jesus said unto the centurion, 'Go thy way; as thou hast believed, so be it done unto thee.'"

Here, in this passage of scripture, we see Jesus marvel at someone's faith. I have never yet met a Christian who did not, somewhere in his secret heart, want to feel that his faith was good enough to gain the attention and approval of God. Here, Jesus gives us the key to making sure this happens every time. Jesus marveled at a simple faith that needed only the Word. The centurion would have gone away disappointed if he had come to Jesus demanding a sign from heaven (as the scribes and Pharisees had done) before he would condescend to believe. Do we want to make our Father God proud of us? We must demand of ourselves that we are going to press forward on nothing but the Word of God.

Church, somehow we have got to get over the idea that whatever we think, whatever we feel, whatever we want, whatever we like, whatever we don't like, whatever agrees with our doctrinal preferences is SOOOOOOO important. We are making the Word of God roll over and play dead in the face of our opinion and desire to be right. Once the Word of God becomes our only bottom line, we will experience the kind of results we have wanted all the time! Furthermore, the things we think we need and the things we expect to happen in our walk with God will change dramatically, as well.

This centurion knew what he wanted, and where to go to get it. He did not know only one thing: What did the Word have to say on the matter? As soon as he found out what the Word had to say, it was a done deal as far as he was concerned—so he went home. Church, once you find out what the Word has to say, you have all the answer you'll ever need on that particular topic. Whatever your problem or challenge, go to the Word, not to find support for your doctrinal stance, but to find God's answer to your need. Stand there, on that answer, and the results God said you could have will be yours—that answer will become your reality.

"Pastor, I don't know the scriptures very well, so I just pray in the name of Jesus, because I know He has promised to answer me if I do. And, you know, I always pray 'if it be thy will!'"

Great. Let's look at some more scriptures.

Philippians 2:9-10 — "Wherefore God also hath highly exalted him, and given him a name which is above every other name: That at the name of Jesus every knee should bow, of things in heaven, and things in earth, and things under the earth."

We had better pray in the name of Jesus! His name is exalted above every other name that is named—anywhere! Then, if it were not enough that His name is exalted, Jesus gave us His name to use when we need to wield His authority in the earth. Through His name we have been given His personal guarantee that we will be heard in the courts of heaven, and that we will be heeded in the halls of hell. Our use of the Name of Jesus is an added guarantee that our prayers will be answered. There is, however, a more important and deeply abiding guarantee than the Name Above All Names.

Psalm 138: 2b — "... for Thou hast magnified Thy Word above all thy name." It is far more important to have God's Word on a matter than to pray about it in the Name of Jesus! Please don't misunderstand me! I believe in praying in the name of Jesus. I pray in the name of Jesus. I expect results in the name of Jesus, but none of us can expect to receive anything from God if we don't know His will. God's Word is His Will—His Will is His Word!! No honest man that ever lived, willed one thing, and said something else.

"Weeelllll, You never know what God's gonna do, Brother."

If we don't know what God's gonna do, it is because of one of two basic things: Either we don't read the Bible, or we don't believe the Bible.

"Yeah, but I can't understand the Bible."

If all else fails, use a dictionary. The Author is quite intelligent, and above-average honest. The words He used, to write His Book, have actual definitions, just like real words.

I used to say the same kinds of things because I honestly didn't understand what I was reading. I didn't understand because everything I read was going through the filter of what I'd been taught. A lot of what I'd been taught was not what the Bible said, but it was based on something in the Bible combined with some experience. When I began to read God's Will as simply as it was intended to be read in the first place, my understanding began to multiply. I had to discard a lot of garbage that had somehow shaped itself into a very unwieldy system of theology. I found that I believed that God hated murder, and yet He Himself would murder, if it suited His mysterious purposes that of course, were far too complex to understand. In the real world, they call that hypocrisy. I found that I believed that God was an amazingly wealthy individual, and yet He somehow expected me to be content with poverty. That He, wealthy, was Holy, and that I, poor, was to be Holy too, through being poor. In the real world, they call that confusing. I found that I believed that God could heal (Jesus did it quite a lot, and apparently enjoyed doing it) yet, for some reason (not possible for me to know), He could not only refuse to heal me, but actually make me sick to teach me a lesson, or get my attention. In the real world, they call that child abuse.

If we own a Bible, we are utterly without excuse. We can turn on our "real world" brain, and read. That's what we do when we read anything else, isn't it? We don't allow our religious filters to render the Six O'clock News unintelligible. Why should we allow those same filters to cloud and confuse the most important Book we will ever hold in our hands?

The cornerstone of an accurate understanding of the most important issue facing the Body of Christ in this hour is the character and nature of God. If you feel that your mind is already made up, and you will not allow a new or different idea to mess with your comfortable theology, just hand this book to someone else and forget it. As we progress further, it's just going to get worse because I'm going to let the air out of some very old and sacred theological balloons. If you are afraid you might get hurt, run now. Let me assure you, I do not in any way intend to hurt you, only to help. If something I say does hurt, be willing to suspend your fear and defensiveness momentarily, the help is on the way. My desire, and the reason I undertook this project in the first place, is for us to become more congruent Christians.

Congruent Christians are productive and happy Christians. Congruent Christians are free. Free to reach their own highest potential in Christ. Free to influence the world around them with all the good God has put in them. Free to carry out the Great Commission without the religious baggage of legalistic bondage. I want us free. I want us whole. Most importantly, God wants us free and whole. Believe His Word. Believe it above all other evidence. Believe it above your own mind and feelings. We must believe it above the attitudes, opinions and feelings of others. We must believe that God is smart enough to say exactly what He means and that He is honest enough to mean exactly what He says. If we believe this, we will come to know the truth, and we will be FREE!!

two
Know Your Enemy, Satan

I know there are a lot of good Christian people who really don't like to talk about the devil. He agrees. The devil doesn't like for us talk about him, unless of course, we are telling someone how powerful he is, and how impossible he is to defeat—he loves that! The problem is that it's not true! He is not all that powerful, and he is very defeatable! By the way—he hates it when people talk like that about him. After all, much like Hollywood, he believes that "image is everything!"

What I would like to do on the next few pages is look into a few verses of Scripture that give us God's idea of what we are to think about the devil. It won't take very long, so don't get nervous. We are about to see that the devil is very easy to understand, and his tricks are a knowable commodity. He has only one real power, and only five tools with which to wield that power. Satan's mission is so simple that it sounds simplistic to describe it. We can learn, with one question, to find out who is at work in our life—Satan or God.

Let's start at the beginning with a statement from God's Word (the truth which sets us free) about Satan and his devices.

2 Corinthians 2:11 says, "Lest Satan should get an advantage of us: for we are not ignorant of his devices." I want to point out several things about this verse: First, the word "lest" is not "least" as I have so often heard it pronounced. Lest is an old English word that means "unless", or "for fear that". The phrase, "lest Satan should get an advantage of us," comes right after Paul teaches about practical forgiving, and it is the reason for that forgiving. If we fail to become good, practical forgivers, Satan, who is surely crazy but not the least bit stupid, will use our hardness of heart to take an advantage over us.

The big thing in this verse that I wanted to point out is the last half, which is the statement of God about you and me, and what we are supposed to know, already. God's Word says, "... we are not ignorant of his devices." The Greek word translated "devices" means "mind, thoughts and purposes." If we will only think about it a little bit, we will see that we really are not ignorant of what is going on in Satan's mind, what his thoughts are, and what his purposes are for our lives. So, what are the thoughts and purposes in the devil's mind for us, as believers?

Ephesians 6:11 says we are to "Put on the whole armor of God, that ye may be able to stand against the wiles of the devil." The Greek word that is translated "wiles," is spelled METHODIA. This is where we get our word "method." In Greek, it means "trickery" or "skillfully laid plans." The devil wants to trick us! If he can fool us into believing something about him that is not true, he has achieved his purpose. You see, he knows, probably better than we do, that we will operate out of our spirit based on what we believe, whether it is right or wrong.

Trickery, or in today's vernacular, sneakiness, is one of the things the devil uses to great effect on Christians. The devil sneaks in on people who are not overly diligent about learning what the Word of God has to say to them. How? If we don't know what God's will is on any given matter, the devil can easily trick us into believing the wrong thing. About God. About ourselves. About the devil.

Example: Brother Burfus J.P.R.D. Ripaticket (fictitious name, could you tell?), who thinks he knows enough and besides, "That dumb pastor, all he ever preaches is 'love your wife,' and besides, I'm more spiritual than he is, anyway" (etc. etc. etc. ad infinitum, ad nauseum), has a heart attack. In the hospital, stretched out flat on his back, tubes and wires everywhere, Burfus picks up the Gideon's Bible and begins to read, possibly for the first time in ten or fifteen years. The Holy Spirit begins to teach him from what he's reading (The Holy Spirit is the teacher of the Church, after all), and Burfus receives a revelation from the Spirit of God. Brother Burfus immediately begins to tell everyone who gets close enough to hear, that now he knows why God knocked him flat and blessed him with that massive heart attack, and enough medical bills to bring on bankruptcy. "God gave me that heart attack so he could teach me a lesson."

"Sounds reasonable to me, Pastor! Why do you think that's the enemy tricking him?"

It is a trick of the enemy because Burfus developed an erroneous conclusion about God, and another one about himself. Burfus concluded that because some good came to him—that is, he received a revelation from the Holy Spirit—that it must have been God who gave him the heart attack that flattened him. Burfus failed to recognize that all revelation comes from the Word of God through the Spirit of God, and that anyone can receive a revelation from the Holy Spirit if they will just spend the time it takes in the Word! The erroneous conclusion Burfus reached about himself was that he was so spiritually stupid and thickheaded that God had to flatten him, just to get his attention.

Burfus failed to recognize that God is still God, and very capable of getting His point across to any of His kids, without smashing them around to make sure they are awake. We have all heard dozens of times, "the Holy Spirit is a Gentleman, and He will not be rude enough to interrupt what you are doing, unless you ask Him." If that is true, why are we so willing to believe that that same Holy Spirit will inflict pain on an unwilling listener, just to make him listen? If that is a Godly thing to do, maybe all pastors should equip their sanctuary chairs with electricity, to make people, who would rather sleep, listen. You think church attendance is small now …

Why do we insist that God use tactics that don't work for us? I find it amazing that the God Who most of the body of Christ thinks they serve is less intelligent, and more cruel, than the average, thick-skulled human! This "trickery" is not the greatest of his powers, nor is it the most valued of his tools. Before we discuss what is, let's take a look at a few other things that Satan uses against the Body of Christ. In 2 Timothy 3:6, 7 we can see three more. "Not a novice, lest being lifted up with pride he fall into the condemnation of the devil. Moreover he must have a good report of them which are without; lest he fall into reproach and the snare of the devil." The three things Satan will use to set a trap for us are condemnation, reproach and snare.

Ordinarily, it is a simple trap, using our own flesh and its desires as bait. He will patiently take the time to talk us into doing something really stupid, all the while telling us how great it's going to be, and how sneaky we are, and how nobody will ever know about it, because we are really careful. The very instant we go ahead and commit that particular sin, the enemy of our soul begins to condemn us, expose us, and bring us into reproach. If Satan can, through this set of tactics, shut us up, and hinder our Christian walk, he has destroyed yet another powerful person, invalidating that person's right and ability to control his (the devil's) behavior.

Please understand: It's not about us, it's about the devil still trying to dethrone and hurt the Father. It's neither about how weak we are nor what a louse we are to fall for such a stupid temptation. We, weak louse that we are, can, on our weakest and lousiest day, speak the Word of God and totally dominate the devil and his plans for our section of the world. Satan has used this set of tactics over and over for thousands of years, and people of higher caliber than you and I have fallen for it, over and over again. So, we must not think it's at all personal and unique with us. Beloved, please understand, we are nothing more to the devil than in the way. He doesn't love us so much he can't stand to lose us and he doesn't hate us at all—he wants to kill us because then he won't have to listen to us any more! He doesn't hate us—he hates God!

The routine of Snare, Condemnation and Reproach, simply works. Why shouldn't he use what works?

"But, Pastor! It's just not fair!!"

Of course it's not fair! Whoever gave us the goofy idea anything was going to be fair? Do we actually expect that the enemy of God, who tried to kick Him off His Own throne, then vowed eternal enmity against Him and His, who has done absolutely nothing but kill, steal and destroy since the day he was thrown out of heaven, who knows that his end is nothing better than eternal torment in eternal chains in eternal fire, who can get closest to God by getting closest to His people—do we actually expect him to be fair in any of his dealings with us???

It is time for each of us, as members of the Body of Christ, to lay aside as much of our foolish, childish thinking as possible, and reach toward maturity, as hard and fast as we can.

Has the devil set a trap for us, and then talked us into walking into it? (The correct answer here is, "Yes.") Did he then condemn us for it (The correct answer again is, "Yes."), and expose us to reproach (Again, the correct answer is, "Yes.")? He probably also convinced us that we were the only ones to do that, didn't he?

NO! He is not telling the truth this time! So we fell for his most trusted "sucker punch". Repent. Get up, and get back to telling the devil where to get off. Yeah, we feel stupid, just like everybody else who has ever fallen for it. If we let feeling stupid keep us from our appointed duties in this world, we have given the devil enough power to effectively stop the plan of God for our life.

It is going to be really tough to stand before the throne of God, holding before us like a dirty diaper the unfulfilled Plan of God, and try to explain to the Great Empowerer that the reason we didn't do anything with His Plan for us is because, "Well, I just kinda felt stupid. Ya know?"

If I were your enemy, and I were invisible to the physical realm in which you move, and I wanted nothing more than to destroy you as completely as possible, do you think I would come to you as myself, or in some kind of disguise? Your first guess is probably disguise. You are right! So, what kind of disguise do you think your enemy uses to greatest effect? Does he come disguised as God? An angel? Another Christian? Maybe. But I think the most effective disguise Satan can use to attack you, is to come to you disguised as ... you!! If we think we are having a particular thought about someone, even though it is negative and un-Christ-like, we will not resist its impression on our mind. If we knew it was an impression from the devil, we wouldn't hesitate to throw the bum out on his ear!

He doesn't want to be thrown out, or stopped in any way, so he comes disguised as us, sounding just like our thoughts, when in reality those thoughts are not ours at all!

"Won't that preacher ever shut up? It's already 12:01!!"

"Here it comes. She's going to deliver the 'You-Never-Listen' lecture, again. Nag. Nag. Nag."

"My boss is so stupid! I'm a lot smarter than he is. Why does the idiot keep passing over me and promoting the dummies I work with?" Etc.

Get the idea? Have we heard anything similar going around in our mind about ourselves, or those around us? Those were not our thoughts!! Those thoughts are not ours until we speak them with our own mouth. You see, the devil is not in charge of our mouth. We alone are in charge of our mouth. Satan is referred to as a "supernatural" being—that is, existing, but not physical—he is not present everywhere all the time. He is not all-knowing. He is not all-powerful.

In actual reality, it is only possible for Satan to know three things about us. First, he knows what we watch and read and hear. Second, he knows what he tells us. And third, he knows what we say. In fact, that's the only way he has of finding out that what he is telling us is getting through. If we will make the mature decision to control our tongue, and not allow anything to pass over it that is not in line with the revealed Will of God, Satan could get the idea that he is no longer getting through to us! Wouldn't it be refreshing to make him confused for a change?

Now we come to Satan's only real power in dealing with the human race. We will see that he has, in actual fact, only the one actual power, and that he uses a mere five tools to exercise that one power.

If I could get you to understand thoroughly one thing at this point, it would be that the devil is not as all-powerful and all-knowing as he has been telling us he is. He is distinctly limited, and his limitations are very much in our favor.

Satan's only real power is sneaky, and he uses it to trap, condemn and bring a believer into reproach. It is, in itself, empowered by the individual believer upon whom it is working. It is, in actual practice, spread abroad and encouraged by believers as much, or more, than it is by devils themselves.

"Well, what is it?"

The devil's only real power is the lie. The first half of Revelation 20:10 tells us: "And the devil that deceived them ... " The Greek word translated "deceived" means "to cause to wander out of the way." In Webster's Dictionary, deception is defined as "... a lie; an untruth; a partial truth designed to incite belief and action for the teller's personal gain." A lie doesn't have to be a blatant attack against the truth. It can be something as simple as a slight nudge off center.

An effective lie doesn't have to get us to fall on our face and worship demons. It is just as effective if it causes us to pray in a manner, which God cannot answer if He is going to maintain His integrity—and He is going to maintain His integrity, no matter what.

"What kind of prayer is it that God can't answer?"

When a Christian prays outside the revealed will of God—His Word, that Christian is asking God to break His Word, and give him/her a special favor, just because the need is so great.

"Lord, If you heal Aunt Bertha, I'll tell everybody!" (A great testimony is sure to make God do the impossible!) Never mind the fact that Aunt Bertha has been telling everybody she comes across that God has allowed her to get cancer because now she is a better Christian.

Several years ago, a man in his mid-seventies came to my door to ask me to pray for him. He had found out several years before that he had cancer, and just recently was told by his doctor that his time was very short. He was told that he would be dead within just a few weeks. He came to my door in tears, weeping out this story: "God called me to preach when I was fourteen years old, and I told Him 'No.' I have felt the pressure of the Holy Spirit on my heart every day since that time, and every day I have told him 'No.' I have heard that people get healed when you pray, and I want you to pray for me. I want you to tell God for me that if He will heal me, I will preach." I told him that I would most assuredly pray, and release my faith for his healing, but he would have to play "Let's Make A Deal" with God all by himself. He left my house a very sad man, because his entire belief in whether or not my prayer for his healing would be answered was based on whether or not I could talk God into taking the "Deal".

Six weeks later that man was dead. Why? Because my prayer for his healing did not work? Not at all. That man believed that cancer came upon him because he was disobedient to the call of God and God was punishing him. Wrong answer!

Ask the average Christian how many of his prayers—specific requests—have received specific answers. The answer is sad. The lie has even permeated Christian practical theology to the point that we have heard from our "spiritual leaders" that "sometimes God says 'Yes,' sometimes God says 'No,' and sometimes God says 'Wait.'" However,

God Himself says in 2 Corinthians 1:20, "For all the promises of God, in him are yea, and in him Amen, unto the glory of God by us." That doesn't sound anything remotely like "No" or "Wait" to me!! Isn't it fascinating that we find it easier to believe some religious-sounding thing, even though it cannot be found in the Word at all, than to believe the simple Word of God?

John 8:44b — "When he speaketh a lie, he speaketh of his own: for he is a liar, and the father of it." Jesus Himself told us that the devil is a liar, and in fact, the originator of lies. Is it possible Jesus may have known a little of what He was speaking about? I believe Jesus knew the devil's operation better than anybody else. He said Satan is a liar!

Remember the excerpt we just read from Revelation 20:10? "The devil that deceived them," is how Jesus referred to Satan. He wasn't called the "devil who harassed them." ("Pray for me, Pastor, the devil's after me!") He is not referred to as the "devil who killed them." (If he could, would we be alive?) He is not called "the devil who made them sick," even though that is something he tries to do, (not as often as he gets blamed for). Our body's own natural defense mechanisms and ordinary, fleshly medicine is constantly defeating him in that arena. The fact that people die from diseases is not so much a testimony to the power of the devil as it is a testimony to the lousy shape we are in. "He is called "the devil that deceived them," as if that were the most important thing for which he was being tossed into the lake of fire."

Does the fact that he has deceived us make you wonder? Or are we among those that think we cannot be deceived? Nobody wants to admit that one, but if we are willing to fight about how right we are and how wrong everyone else is, we have been deceived!!

"But Pastor, I've been taught this way all my life!"

I wonder if the Pharisees believed anything contrary to what Jesus was teaching, and I wonder if they had believed it all their lives. Hmmm. Having a desire to be right and theologically accurate very possibly makes us more vulnerable to the devil's deceptions. With our own willingness to condemn others for being theologically inaccurate, we can impress ourselves with how theologically accurate we are. Of course, it never occurs to us that we have become our own standard of accuracy.

Most Christians believe they use the Bible as their standard.

Have we noticed that everybody says that? And on the heels of noticing that, have we noticed how many differing opinions there are about virtually everything the Bible says? Take, for example, the rapture. One viewpoint says it's going to happen before the tribulation (my favorite). One viewpoint says it's going to happen in the middle of the tribulation. One viewpoint says it's going to happen at the end of the tribulation. One viewpoint says it's not going to happen at all. One viewpoint even says that the sinners are going to be taken out of the way, and therefore there will be no tribulation at all! Now, the truly interesting thing about this theological hodge-podge, is this: they all use the same few verses to prove their point!!! If that were not enough, they will all fight for their right to be right, subsequently assuming everyone else is wrong.

If deception is Satan's only real power, how does it work, why does he use it, and what does he use to bring it about?

The answers to all these questions are found in Mark 4:14-20. Let's start by answering the question, "Why?"

Verses 14-15 — "The sower soweth the word. And these are they by the wayside, where the word is sown; but when they have heard, Satan cometh immediately, and taketh away the word that was sown in their hearts."

Why does Satan come to deceive us? Because of the Sovereign Word of a Sovereign God that has been planted in our heart. Whatever kind of attack we come under, we must know this: it is not personal. The devil doesn't hate us. He hates God. He isn't trying to stop us. He's trying to stop the plan of God. He isn't after us. He is after the Word of God, which, when mixed with faith, controls him.

Read verses 3-9, and see the parable of the sower (Parable of the Word is more accurate). In verse 4, the fowls of the air came after the seed (Word); they didn't attack the soil (people). So please, tenderhearted Christian, don't think the devil's maneuverings in our lives are personal—we aren't that important to him—we're just in the way.

In verses 16 and 17, we see the first two of the devil's five tools that he uses to either destroy the Word in our heart, or make it unproductive. "And these are they likewise which are sown on stony ground" (read 'hardness of heart'); "who, when they have heard the word, immediately receive it with gladness; and have no root in themselves, and so endure but for a time: afterward, when affliction or persecution arises for the word's sake, immediately they are offended." The emphases and parentheticals are mine, not God's, but I wished to show you a point or two as we read the text of scripture. Hard heartedness, and what's-in-it-for-me-ism produces more "offended-ness" than anything else that comes to mind right now. It is important to note that these people did receive the Word "with gladness," but they had no "root" in themselves with which to feed the Word (that's what roots do). After they endured for a time, Satan's first two tools, which he uses to destroy the Word, came into play.

Affliction (we'll talk about this one in greater depth, in a later chapter) is translated from a Greek word, which means, "trouble." To me, the best modern kind of word to use, to make this one understandable, is the word "problems." Have you got any problems? How do you feel about them? How do they make you feel about yourself? How do our problems affect the way we deal with those around us? How do our problems affect the way we pray, and relate to God? Problems were designed by the devil to uproot the Word of God in our heart.

"Do all my problems come from the devil?"

Nope.

Some of them were here before we came along, and we just stepped in them (like so many cow patties). Some of them we invented ourselves, because of hard spots in our heart. The important thing to understand about problems is not who to blame—the important thing to understand is what they are doing to our walk in the Word of God. Are our problems causing us to blame God? Are they causing us to condemn ourselves? Are they causing us to be offended with the people around us? All of these responses are the wrong ones, and will lead us to erroneous conclusions. If that is what our problems are producing in us, the devil is getting exactly what he wants. We have given up on the Word of God to bring its power to bear in our situation. We have accepted the LIE that these problems are the tool of God to get our attention, and teach us a lesson. Our problems are indeed a tool, but that tool is not God's.

Persecution is the second one of these tools mentioned in verse 17. The Greek word literally means, "pursue." The best modern word I have found to help me in my understanding of this word, is the word "pressure." Most people in this day and age think of Persecution in terms of Blood and Guts, being Fed to the Lions, and Killed for your Faith. Not much of that is happening to us, is it? However, everybody understands the word pressure or stress. If pressure over money can get us to abandon our stand of faith, and do the dishonest thing instead, Satan's tool has accomplished its desire—we have abandoned the Word of God as if He would never bring it to pass for us. Pressure is not God's way of getting our attention; it is the devil's way of giving us a heart attack or a stroke. Medical science has long since concluded that strokes and heart attacks are brought on by a combination of things, the biggest of which is stress.

In Mark 4:18 and 19, we see the other three tools the devil uses to great effect in the lives of believers. "And these are they which are sown among thorns; such as hear the word, And the cares of this world, and the deceitfulness of riches, and the lusts of other things entering in, choke the word, and it becomes unfruitful."

The first two, the enemy uses to try to completely destroy the Word in our heart. These next three, the devil uses to simply make the Word unproductive.

"Why would he want to do that?"

Simple.

Whether it is destroyed, or just not producing, God's Word, in either case, cannot dominate and control the enemy in his desires for our life. Again, it isn't personal, the devil just doesn't like to be controlled—and the Word of God in the heart and mouth of a child of God is the only thing that controls him.

Before we take a look at each of the three, I want us to see that each of these must "enter in" before it can make the Word—"it" not "you"—unfruitful. How do we let these things "in?" They "enter in" when we pay more heed to, and talk more about them than to the Word that is being sown in our heart. We wouldn't do to a garden in our back yard what we do to our heart—weed out the produce and cultivate the weeds! It doesn't make sense to encourage our doubts and doubt the Word of God! We must encourage our faith! We must purposely doubt our fears and doubts! Cultivate the Word and weed out the thorns of unbelief! Not even God can do that for us. If He could, doesn't He love us enough that He would have already have done it? We must do it on our own.

The Greek word translated "cares" means "distractions." A distraction is something that takes our focus off its intended target. What is the intended focus of every believer if not the Word of God? This world has a seemingly infinite number of distractions for unwary Christians—some of them are even really good things. If Satan can distract us with "caring" about something to the point that it chokes out our desire to please God, obey His Word, and bear fruit for Him— Mission Accomplished: Tool Three.

The Greek word translated "deceitfulness" is defined as "having the ability to cheat." What ability do riches have to cheat? None, in and of themselves. Money has neither personality nor character. It is neither good nor bad. It does not do good or bad things by itself. The person who understands what God thinks about money cannot be corrupted by it. If money, all by itself, could corrupt us, the devil himself would make us rich! If poverty is so good for us, and makes us so wonderfully spiritual, why does the devil let us have so much of it, so freely? The only thing that gives riches the ability to cheat us, is what we think about money.

Before I met Jesus, I was on drugs, and lived on the streets of the western United States and Mexico, for about three years. During that time, I could have walked fifteen minutes in any direction and found a hit man for as little as fifty dollars. The person who can kill for fifty dollars has been deceived by money—not because of money, but because of what they think about money. Very few of the wealthy people I know are deceived by the way they think about money. Most of the truly poor people I know are deceived by the way they think about money. If you have ever thought that everything would be better if you just had more money, you have been deceived. You have been cheated by the thought of riches if you have given up believing that God will provide for you and have decided to worry it out yourself.

The Biblical word "lust" has, in these days, confused many

members of the Body of Christ. All too often, we tend to think of lust in terms of sex, but that is a very limited application. The Greek term translated "lust" in this verse means "to set the heart upon.' We have set our hearts upon many things that have nothing at all to do with sex. Please understand. To set our heart upon any of the things of this life, in a proper, controlled, and balanced manner, is not a bad or sinful thing at all. It becomes "lust" when our desire has jumped the fence of proper boundaries, and we have set our heart upon a thing or person, in opposition to, or beyond the limits of, the Word of God. Lusts of other things, entering in to our hearts, chokes out the normal and proper growth of the Word in our hearts and lives. We can't be overboard on something, and expect the Word to grow in us, or to cause us to grow, at the same time. God has never blessed imbalance, and He's not going to start now.

These three tools, the Cares of this world, the Deceitfulness of riches, and the Lusts of other things, are not Satan's Word Destroyers like the first two tools we looked at. They are his Word Chokers. They won't destroy the Word in us; they will simply make it unproductive. The Word of God was designed by its Author to produce when it gets planted in a human heart. Over the course of time, the devil figured out just a few things that can cause that productivity to stop.

I don't believe that the devil really cares a lot whether the Word in us is destroyed, or just unfruitful. He just cares that we don't end up telling him where to get off. You see, Satan is an outlaw. A criminal, if you prefer. His desires are the same as all criminals everywhere—"Don't tell me what to do, and don't try to control me!" We can look at what we understand of the Mafia to see a barely restrained criminal viewpoint. They might control themselves, for whatever their purposes are, up to a point, but nobody else should dare try to control them.

The marvelous thing about the Word of God is that it not only equips us to control the devil and shake off his controls on us, it gives us the power to do it as well. God is really smart to come up with something so simple as the Word of God and make it do so many things, all at once!!!!

Now, I would like to take a look at a few other verses that deal with the nature and character of the enemy. Jesus taught us what we need to know about the devil, without getting all spooky or demon-conscious.

John 10:10 says, "The thief cometh not, but for to steal, and to kill, and to destroy: I am come that they might have life, and that they might have it more abundantly."

Isn't it interesting that Jesus calls Satan a thief? Is something being stolen in our life? The devil did it. Is a friendship or a blessing being killed in our life? The devil did it. Is something being destroyed in our life? The devil did it.

"Oh, Pastor! That's just too simplistic. Nothing can be that cut and dried."

You could be right. However, it seemed to be a good enough explanation for Jesus. Looking at it objectively, I honestly don't think I am any smarter than He is. Therefore, I conclude: If I am no smarter than Jesus, maybe, just maybe, His explanations should be quite sufficient for me.

If we are willing to look at life simply, the way Jesus did, it is plain enough to see that if it is bad (being stolen, killed, or destroyed), it is from the devil, and if it is good (in the widest sense of the word), and abundant-life-filled, it is from God. Resist, rebuke and flee from one and give praise for the other. Simple enough? Good. Too simple? Tough. Either we learn to think simply, in real-world terms, or we must expect the devil to steam-roll us at every turn. Simple.

In Matthew 4:3, we see the devil referred to as the "tempter." We are going to discuss this more fully in a later chapter, but for now, let's just look at the definition of the word "tempt" or "temptation" so we can see exactly what it is the devil does in his role as "tempter."

In studying this word in my Strong's Concordance (I recommend that you get one for yourself, so you can study these things on your own), I discovered some definitions, which shed a lot of light on my understanding. The Greek words translated "tempt" or "temptation" are defined as follows: "to test," "to examine," "to scrutinize," "to put to the test," "to put to proof," "to provoke," "to assay." Isn't it interesting that none of these words means, "to try to get you to do something sinful?" Yet that is exactly the idea we have of what it means to be "tempted."

We have, somehow, picked up the idea that "temptation" means that the devil is trying to get us to do something sinful, which of course, we don't want to do. I have looked and looked, and there doesn't seem to be any Biblical word that means that. The Biblical word "temptation" simply means "to test or examine." Has anyone ever told you all about the rotten thing they were going through, and wrapped up with a conclusion that they were being put to the test by God so He could "see what kind of stuff I'm made of?"

If God knows everything (and He does), why would He need to poke around on us like a laboratory rat, to "see what we're made of?" Somehow, our thinking has gotten all messed up. We think temptations are bad because they come from the devil (that's what the Book says), but tests and trials are good because they come from God (that's not what the Book says). All along, they are the same thing, coming from the same Greek word, and from the same source. If God were to "provoke" us, He would be guilty of breaking His own command to fathers in Ephesians 6:4: "Fathers, do not provoke your children to wrath." To "assay" means, "to put through all kinds of tests for the purpose of discovering intrinsic value or worth." The Scripture says Satan does that, yet we have been taught it is God who is doing that to us.

That's another one of those things that makes you go "Hmmm" (or at least it should).

In the next chapter, we are going to take a look at the character and nature of our Father, God. This is by no means a complete or definitive study, just a brief look. A complete or definitive study of such a subject is impossible, and if it were possible to do it, it could not be lifted without a crane. I just want to touch on some of the more vital points of His character and nature, mainly to try to dispel some of the confusion that exists in the minds of many in the Body of Christ.

It is important to point out that the Word of God is very important to God, and should be to us. If God says something once, in His Word, we can stake our life on it, without question. If He says something twice in His Word, we'd better listen. If God thinks enough of a thing to say it as many times as three in His Word, WE'D BETTER LISTEN!!!!

With that in mind, read on.

three
Know Your Father, God

As I said, I will cover only a portion of this topic, touching on only a few of the more salient points.

God is love. I John 4:8b — "... God is love." This is probably one of the most used and least understood verses dealing with the Father's character and nature. The Greek word translated "love" in this passage is the word "agape," (pronounced uh-GAH-pay"). There are all kinds of definitions for this word and most of them are pretty good. My personal favorite is this: Agape is completely one directional giving, without hint, thought, or demand of return. If God demanded that we return the love He has given us, He would be bitterly disappointed all the time. If that were the kind of love He gave, it would not be possible for Him to give His love a second time, until we fully returned it the first time. Needless to say, we would be finished.

Notice, this verse does not say that love is something God has—it is who He is. The Agape love of God is an integral part of His very nature. Massive books could be and have been written on the subject without ever scratching the surface. For our purposes here, suffice it to say that the core of His nature is love, and that love is manifested in a variety of ways. Let's look at some of them.

God is merciful. The Hebrew term that is translated "merciful" means "having compassion." It is interesting to note that the Greek term translated "merciful" also means "having compassion." The dictionary definition of the English word "merciful" means "filled with tender, loving mercy and kindness." This sounds a lot like compassion to me. Compassion is an outward-directed motivation, which does not work to get its own needs met, but rather seeks to meet the needs of someone else.

Psalms 86:5 says, "For thou Lord, art good, and ready to forgive; and plenteous in mercy unto all them that call upon thee."

The word "plenteous" means, "having more than enough, with plenty to spare." It would take far too much time and space here, to go into greater detail about the importance of understanding God's mercy. Let it be sufficient to say that the greater your revelation of His mercy, the greater will be your ability to walk in love consistently.

I have been accused of preaching too much Grace and not enough Holiness. When my Pastor asked me how I felt about that, I told him I felt that I was doing my job the way it needs to be done—if you don't have an understanding of God's Grace, you'll not walk in real Holiness. You'll just be legalistic. God's Mercy and His Grace are different, yet intertwined and interdependent. When the Bible says that God is plenteous in mercy, I simply have to believe it is true, that there is more than enough mercy to go around. Let's look at a few other verses about God's mercy.

Deuteronomy 7:9 — "Know therefore that the Lord thy God, He is God, the faithful God, which keepeth covenant and mercy with them that love Him and keep His commandments to a thousand generations."

He is not the Average God, the Regular God, or the "You-never-know-what's-gonna-happen-next" God. He is the Faithful God, who keeps His Word and His mercy to a thousand generations.

We're not out of generations yet!!! Hallelujah!!

Remember the end of the last chapter? I said that if God says something once in His Word, we could stake our life on it. If He says something twice in His Word, we'd better listen. If God thinks enough of a thing to say it as many as three times in His Word, we'd better LISTEN!!! This pairing of words, "mercy and truth" occurs not less than eight times in the Bible. Do we get the feeling that maybe God is trying to make a point? We have sort of an idea about what mercy is, but what does the Bible say about "truth?" If we can figure out what, from God's perspective, constitutes "truth," we may have a foundation for figuring out anything else, about which we desire to know the "truth?"

I think so, too.

So, what is "truth?"

In John 17:17b, Jesus said, speaking to the Father, "Thy Word is truth." As a part of a conversation He had with the Father, Jesus, the most honest individual in the entire Universe, said that the Word of God is truth. Notice, He didn't say it contains truth, nor did He say it is A truth. When God says, of anything, "this" is "that," He means that those words are interchangeable, and that interchanging them will not in any way, scripturally, spiritually, morally, ethically, legally or horticulturally, damage the statement. Wherever you see the word "truth" in the Bible, you can read it, "the Word of God" and you will be completely accurate every time.

So, why are "mercy" and "truth" tied together? Your guess is as good as mine. I believe it is because God wants us to understand that, just as He Himself is full of mercy, so too is His Word. No matter how many well-meaning Christians try to employ the Word of God as a battering ram to beat us and put us into religious bondage to "do's" and "don'ts" (even scriptural ones), the Word of God itself will always treat us with mercy. Now, don't misunderstand. The Word has some very hard things to say, but those things are never condemnatory nor are they ever cruel. God is love, and we can't beat someone up in love. God is full of mercy, and we cannot condemn someone, nor put him or her in bondage, with mercy.

Hebrews 4:16 says, "Let us therefore come boldly unto the throne of grace, that we may obtain mercy, and find grace to help in time of need."

The word "obtain" is just a $49 word for "get." If we can reach out and "get" something, just because you have decided you want it, that must mean it is available to be "got." Not only are we told we can "get" mercy, but when we get it, we can do it "boldly." God did not create us to be some little shrinking, stammering, cringing, whining, pitiful wimp who needs to be afraid of Him (or anybody else, for that matter). He made us His children!! He made us with rights (that's what "righteous" means)! When we made Jesus Lord of our life, we became a part of God's family! We must let ourselves see Him as His Word says He really is. We must let ourselves see us as His Word says we really are. We must have enough courage to make God's Word our only bottom line, and we will see changes come into our life that we have never even imagined.

"But, Pastor! How can I make the Word my only bottom line?"

Look in the Word until you find something about you. Make sure it is about YOU and about what God has done for you in Jesus. Then begin to speak of it in the present tense, as if it were already a practical reality in your life. For example, when I began to apply this to my own life, I determined that the root cause of most of my problems was anger. I then determined that the Biblical answer to my anger problem was the Love of God. I took 1 Corinthians 13:4-8, and made them personal, speaking those words out of my mouth, out loud many, many times a day. Because God is Love, and because He lives inside me, and because I am born again by that love, I personalized these verses until I was speaking about myself the same way God spoke about Job (more info to follow on that). I said, "I am patient. I am kind. I am not envious. I do not promote myself, and I am not prideful. I do not behave rudely. I do not seek my own way. I cannot be provoked into actions unbecoming of Jesus. I think no evil. I think only the best of everyone. I do not rejoice when evil wins out, but I rejoice when the truth prevails. I bear up under everything. I wholeheartedly believe the Word of God in everything. I hope for the best in every circumstance. I endure all things, good and bad, and I never fail." There are several Biblical principles involved in this process which we will discuss in upcoming chapters, but for now, just do it.

Making the Word our bottom line requires an attitude adjustment. We must take as "truth" what God says, even in the face of contrary evidence and feelings. There are times when Christians don't "feel" saved, but they have accepted the fact that what the Bible says about their salvation is more true than their feelings, so they continue to speak of themselves as being saved. Jesus didn't say, "Thy Word is truth, unless of course, my emotions or my circumstances are telling me something else." I for one am grateful He didn't. We must speak what the Word says about us. We must do it consistently, do it constantly, and we will see ourselves begin to change, right before our very own eyes! Now, that's exciting!

In 1 Chronicles 16:34 we see another of those "if God says something once ..." phrases. It says, "O give thanks unto the Lord; for he is good and his mercy endureth forever." Wow! He is good and His mercy endures forever! This phrase is used, in the Old Testament alone, no less that 43 times!!! Can we hear God trying to make a point? His mercy is never going to run out, and it doesn't make any difference what we do, it isn't going to surprise God, nor is it going to make Him so angry He breaks His own Word, just so He can getcha!! Listen, Baby, if God was ever gonna getcha for messing up, we have already messed up enough to be got.

God is good. This passage of scripture says He is good. I looked up that word in my handy-dandy Strong's Concordance, and I was impressed with the definition. (I'm probably lots easier to impress than you), but here it is: "good = good in the widest sense and application." I knew you'd like it. Just think of it this way: If something can be thought of as good, thank God for it.

"Why?"

Because James 1:17 says, "Every good (same word) gift and every perfect gift is from above, and cometh down from the Father of lights, with whom is no variableness, neither shadow of turning." If a thing or circumstance is intrinsically good, in and of itself, (even if it isn't particularly sPiriTUaL), thank God for it. If it takes a lot of mental gymnastics to find something good, and it is only on the outskirts of the thing in question, don't thank God for it, because He didn't give it to you. When I got in the car accident that cost me two of my fingers, I thanked God for the car wreck. I had been taught that God gives people stuff like that to get their attention, and teach them a lesson. I thanked Him for the wreck, for mangling my fingers so badly they needed to be amputated, for destroying my father's pickup, and for destroying my ability to provide for my family for nearly a whole year. He had my attention, and I was ready to learn anything! What did I learn? Not one solitary thing!! Boy, did God ever miss a perfectly great opportunity to do His thing! Four years later, when I finally began to hear from God again, the first thing He said was,

"I didn't give you the car wreck. I saved your life."

The lights came on!! All of a sudden it hit me! No matter how you look at it, car wrecks are not good. Having a mangled hand and losing fingers to the surgeon's knife is not good. The destruction of my dad's pickup truck (his only vehicle at the time) was not good.

Being unable to provide for my family was not good. I lived. That's good. Nobody else was hurt as badly as they could have been. That's good! Because of the things I had been taught about the character and nature of God, I was thanking God for something He hadn't done and I was not thanking Him for what He had done. When I realized that God is good in the widest sense and application of the term, it suddenly made no sense of any kind to thank Him for something it is not possible for Him to give. Do you realize that if God were to give you a disease, He would have to steal it first? He doesn't have any diseases!! That is the good in the good news!

God is a blesser. The next part of God's character I want to look at is the fact that He is a blesser. Remember as we go through these passages of scripture: If God thinks enough of something to say it once, we can stake our life on it. If He says it twice, we'd better listen. If He cares enough to say the same thing three times in His Word, we'd better pay attention!! The Bible says, "God BLESSED them" no less than 58 times!! Fifty-Eight times!! Is there a point here? Please understand: God does not throw His words around carelessly the way we do. God believes that what He has to say is important enough to be believed.

In Genesis 1:22, we read how God goes about blessing: "And God blessed them, SAYING ..." He blesses us through His own Word! He did it that way in creation and He does it that way today. No matter how badly we may need or want Him to do it differently, He is still God. It seems to me that it would be more important for us to align ourselves with Him than for us to expect Him to align Himself with us.

Ephesians 1:3 says, "Blessed be the God and Father of our Lord Jesus Christ, who hath blessed us with all spiritual blessings in heavenly places in Christ:"

The Father hath (past tense) blessed us! We're not doing "take-a-number-please" WAITING to be blessed—we are blessed right now! And if that were not enough, He has blessed us with all (not some, not a few, not just the important ones, not just the ones that make us look good) spiritual blessings.

I looked up the word "spiritual" in my handy-dandy Strong's Concordance and I was surprised by the definition. It means "non-carnal, or supernatural." Isn't it amazing it doesn't mean you have to wait until you reach heaven to possess it? "Non-carnal" is simply that which the flesh doesn't lust after. It says nothing at all about whether or not the flesh can touch it. As for the word "supernatural," here's the dictionary's definition: "Outside, or exceeding the laws of nature; miraculous: that which is outside the usual course of nature." Nowhere in the definition, either in the Greek language, or in the English language, does it mean "just in the spirit realm, never touching the physical."

Let's be careful that we don't take a perfectly good, honest word, and "spiritualize" the life and the power of God right out of it. I'm quite sure God is smart enough to say exactly what He means, and honest enough to mean exactly what He says. You know, the Bible is a very simple book, if it is approached simply. On the other hand, it does not give up its secrets to the casual observer. It says seek and you will find, knock and it shall be opened unto you. Seeking and knocking in the Word of God does not come naturally to anybody—it is a discipline, which later turns into a hunger for more.

The Bible also says, in 2 Peter 1:3, "According as His divine power hath given unto us all things that pertain to life and godliness, through the knowledge of Him that hath called us to glory and virtue:"

God, the Blesser, hath (past tense) given us something. Notice, it doesn't say He has given some of us, or the really spiritual ones of us, or the truly worthy ones of us—He has already (past tense) given these things to U S! All of us! Each of us! Regardless of us! What did He give to us? All Things—not a few, not some, not the most important, not the basics, not the most decidedly spiritual, and not just enough to get you squeaking through the gates of heaven—All Things that pertain to life and godliness. Is there anything else? What is there that could possibly be called a blessing from God that does not pertain to either life or godliness? I can't think of one single thing. So, God the Blesser provided all these things. How did He provide it, and how does He get it across to us in the daily practicalities of our lives? "... through the knowledge of Him ... " That sounds amazingly similar to the Word of God! Where do we find the knowledge of Him? The Word! If we look elsewhere for the knowledge of the Lord, we will most certainly end up goofier than we ever dreamed possible. In fact this is the main reason for the bad reputation enjoyed by some Charismatics. They have begun an experience and a relationship with the Holy Spirit, and they end up thinking that, just because they are "Spirit-filled," everything they think must be from God, and they couldn't possibly be wrong. It is a sad thing to find someone who thinks the only voice they could possibly hear is the infallible voice of God. Anyone who believes that is setting himself up for a grand failure, and for introducing a lot of hurt and confusion into their section of the Body of Christ. God the Blesser has given us all things that pertain to life and godliness—total spirituality and infallibility do not happen to be among them.

Well, there, it happened. I stopped teaching and started meddling again.

God is our Provider. Another aspect of the character and nature of God I would like to take a look at is the fact that He is our Provider. Now, we all know that He provides all the spiritual blessings there are, but it seems there is a large section of the Body of Christ that has somehow ended up with the idea that that's all there is. Once again, we need to be admonished to put our brain in gear as we read these verses and as we discuss the possibility that God may not be too nervous with the thought of money.

Deuteronomy 8:18 says, "But thou shalt remember the Lord thy God: for it is he that giveth thee the power to get wealth, that he may establish his covenant, which he sware unto thy fathers, as it is this day."

I looked up the Hebrew word that is translated "wealth" in this verse, and it means, "a force, whether of men, means, or other resources, of wealth, valor, strength or virtue." If you pay attention to the world around you, you will have to admit that the Golden Rule is very much in effect in the world's system—"He Who Has the Gold Makes the Rules." Why does the world poor-mouth the church? Because we have told them that God expects us to be poor. I have never understood a pastor preaching against prosperity, then receiving an offering.

The verse we just read says we are to remember the Lord our God, and that He is the one that gives us power (Hebrew word means "vigor, force, ability, capacity, strength, wealth, substance") to get wealth.

There ain't no free lunch. God has given you the vigor, strength and ability to get wealth and power, but He doesn't anoint nor bless gambling or laziness. We must get rid of that welfare-mindedness, arise from our cushy little tookus and work if we expect God to bless our finances. God gave the Israelites the Promised Land, but they had to whip all its inhabitants, including a few really tough giants, to get it.

Why would God want to give us the power to get wealth? So we could be fat and sassy, and show off all our stuff? So we could prove to people by the amount of stuff we have that we are more spiritual than they are?

NO!!

The verse we just read says He does it to establish His covenant—which is His WORD. If God gives us the power to get wealth, and He does, He does it for one purpose only—the Gospel. I get so weary with people who try to play "Let's Make a Deal" with God concerning their finances.

"As soon as I hit the big one, I'm gonna give to your ministry, Pastor."

"I want to give you a Million Dollars, Brother!"

"As soon as I get this promotion, I'm gonna start tithing. Maybe you ought to pray for me to get that big check! (heh, heh)"

"I can't afford it right now, Pastor, but I'm gonna start giving as soon as I get my Income Tax money back, if it's enough. Maybe you oughta pray."

Now, there is a better than even chance I might swallow a bunch of sheep dip like that, because I'm basically gullible, and maybe a little stupid. What really fractures me, though, is when I find people who actually believe that God is ignorant enough to be motivated by that kind of rhetoric. Whatever happened to good, old-fashioned honesty? Honesty with God, even when you don't look so good doing it, will always prove to be the best move. Honesty with yourself only increases the respect you have for God, and His Word, because you find that He loves you anyway.

"So, alright, Pastor, you say God is supposed to be my provider, but it isn't looking too great right now—how is this supposed to work?"

Let's see what the Word has to say on the matter.

Joshua 1:8, in the King James Bible I use says, "This book of the law shall not depart out of thy mouth; but thou shalt meditate therein day and night, that thou mayest observe to do according to all that is written therein: for then thou shalt make thy way prosperous, and then thou shalt have good success."

I want to point out a few things as we go through this verse, a bit at a time.

First, the verse says "this book of the law." Are we dealing with laws, rules and regulations here? Does this apply to just the first five books of the Bible, or can we apply it to the whole Bible? When Joshua wrote this verse, they had no more than the first five books of the Bible. When Joshua referred to the "book of the law," he was referring to all they had—the whole thing. The fact that there is more now than just the first five books is nothing more than a blessing to you and me, because it gives us more of a backlog of answers to draw from as we seek to get the specific answers we need for ourselves. As for whether or not this is about a list of rules, regulations, do's and don't's, the answer is a flat and patent no! If God were a legalist, legalism would work in changing the lives of people. It does not. So why is the Bible referred to as a book of the law? To understand that, you must first ask yourself what a law is.

The best definition of the word "law" I have ever heard is this: A law is something that works every time. We don't speak of gravity as a truth, we speak of it as a law—it works every time. There are other laws that work every time they are put to work, that may, for a brief time, supersede the law of gravity, but good old gravity works every time. The laws of aerodynamics will keep an airplane in the air, as long as the forces of thrust, and lift with an airfoil are kept in motion, but if you wonder whether or not gravity is still working, just step outside. Even if you are an aerospace engineer, you will experience the all-pervading realities of the law of gravity. In the world of physics, the laws of aerodynamics are called "superceding laws"—that is they will hold another, perhaps greater, law at bay, and they will function perfectly so long as they are applied properly. The laws of aerodynamics that keep a Frisbee in the air for long distances will not work on a handkerchief, or a piece of paper. Make the shape of the paper into that of an airplane, and it could outdistance even the best of Frisbees. Shape the handkerchief into a parachute and it will settle to the ground with much more grace and ease than any Frisbee ever could.

God's Word is stuffed with His power. His power makes His words into superceding laws—laws that will work every time, if they are applied properly. If you don't know how to apply them properly, keep reading. We'll cover that soon.

The next phrase says we should keep the Word of God so that it "shall not depart out of thy mouth:" This tells me that the mouth of a believer is a place of primary importance when it comes to receiving from God. Having God's Word in your mouth is, according to what I understand, essential to being able to find out what God expects you to do. We'll cover more as we continue, but let it suffice for now to say that keeping the Word in our mouth is a must.

"But Pastor, how often do I have to do this?"

Twice a day—"day and night."

"But Pastor, that's impossible!"

I knew that. There is even an outside possibility that maybe even God knew that.

So, why would God say something like that? Simple. To tell us first, that it is not a matter of how many times we do it, or how apparently hard it is for us, nor is it a matter of keeping score until we have paid a big enough price before He finally forks over. And secondly, to tell us to just keep at it all the time, as often as is possible for us and don't let up for any reason until we have in our hot little hand the results we have been needing and seeking from God's Word.

"... but thou shalt meditate therein day and night ... "

"Oooooooh, Pastor! That meditation stuff is weird, and occultic, and, and, and, well, it just ain't Christian."

If it isn't Christian, I wonder why God commanded us to do it day and night. Could it be possible that the concept of meditation was God's idea first and the Satanists and the New-Agers have perverted it? Could it be possible that God's way of meditating His Word is even more powerful than the Devil, and his way of meditating? Oooooh!

Now, there's a new idea—God's having more power than the devil and all his bizarre bag of tricks. Can it be? If we ask the average Christian what his theology teaches, he'll tell us, "Of course, God's

Word is much more powerful than anything the devil could possibly come up with!" However, if you observe the average Christian's lifestyle, it will tell you he is scared spitless of the devil, afraid of everything that somebody said may be demonic, and he doesn't trust God, nor believe the bare facts of the Word, as they are laid out in black and white.

I looked up the word "meditate" in my handy-dandy Strong's Concordance and it means "to mutter," "to chew over, as a cud." You know, in teaching the Biblical concepts of meditation of the Scriptures, the one thing I have heard most often from people is that they "don't know how" to meditate the Word of God. Let me ask you this: Have you ever had lessons in worrying? Did you take "Worry 101," or "Fret and Stew 253" in college? I thought not. Why? Because that mental action comes naturally, doesn't it? We don't have to work up a good worry, that particular mental activity seems to produce itself with very little effort on our part. We have never had to get organized and plan out our next fretting session. It came naturally. Meditating the Word of God is exactly the same mental action as worry—we chew on it over and over and over and we mutter about it all day long—we let it consume our mind and attention. Have you noticed that you can do that and work at the same time? It must be that we have a lot more talent and ability at our disposal than we are admitting.

What is the purpose of all this muttering? "... that thou mayest observe to do according to all that is written therein ..." Why meditate the Word of God? So we can see what the Word tells us to do. Please understand: God would much rather have us obedient to one verse of scripture, than able to quote the whole Bible from beginning to end, yet not do what it says to do.

What then, is the purpose of doing what the Word says to do? "... then thou shalt make thy way prosperous, and then thou shalt have good success." It is God's character and nature to provide for us a means of achieving good success and prosperity. God is not a spiritual welfare department, nor is He a financial welfare department. If we have guts enough to do what God tells us to do in the scriptures, He will show us how to work, and how to handle our money wisely, and how to live in godly prosperity. If we have guts enough to do what God tells you to do in the scriptures, then, and not before, we will have what God said we could have, and nothing less.

Philippians 4:19 — "But my God shall supply all your need according to His riches in glory by Christ Jesus."

I have heard well-meaning Christian leaders say, in reference to this passage of Scripture, "It says right here that God will give you needs so that He can be glorified in your life. The fact that you have needs is a blessing from God."

The fact that we have needs is not a blessing from God; it is a testimony to the fact that we are here, and still alive. Do you understand how twisted it is to think God is dumping the celestial manure spreader on us, to teach us something or to get some glory for Himself? The Bible says God will supply our needs, so He gives us needs, so He can supply them???? Get Serious!! If God says He will supply our needs, it is because we obviously already have them, and because it is His nature to desire to take care of us. There is enough garbage around. God doesn't need to engineer any just for us. If He were doing it to make us strong, as some have said, why are we not strong yet? Haven't we had enough "opportunities for growth" thrown at us that have nearly killed us? What's the matter? Are we stupid or something? Can't we get what God is trying to get across to us? Listen. God is a Big Boy. He knows where we live, and He knows how to talk to us. We are His children. We are not Igor, his Laboratory Idiot. If God were going to getcha, we'd already be got. It would be all over for us by now.

The verse in Philippians we just read, also says He will supply our needs according to a certain measure—"according to His riches in glory," and in a certain manner—"by Christ Jesus." Does the Father have any riches in glory? Take out your Bible, and read the 21st chapter of the Revelation, and see for yourself. The streets and the buildings are all made of gold so pure you can see right through it like glass. Each of the twelve gates is made up of one giant pearl! Where did God find that oyster?? God used diamonds, emeralds, rubies, and all kinds of precious and semi-precious stones as gravel in the making of the wall around the city. The guy ain't doin' too bad! I'll bet He probably doesn't even have to worry about the electric company sending Him a shut-off notice or anything! He probably even has His Visa card paid off. Wow!! It is with the same measure that He is rich that he meets our needs. So, why aren't we rich? We'll talk about that in just a bit—read on.

Part of our lack of understanding and therefore our lack of receiving, comes from the fact that we really don't have much of a picture of who He is, and what He has given us in Jesus.

Romans 8:32 says, "He that spared not his own son, but delivered him up for us all, how shall he not with him also freely give us all things?"

Do we honestly think that the "all things" referred to here are just spiritual? Are all those things just the stuff we are going to receive when we get to heaven? If they are, why? Why would God put us in a world where there are needs all around us, and not give us what it takes to meet those temporal needs now? If it is all being saved for heaven, then heaven must be a very materialistic place. Hmmm?

"But Pastor, are you telling me I am supposed to be rich?"

I would, in no way, do that to you. I would, on the other hand, show you what the Bible says and politely request that we clean out the religious cobwebs and figure it out for ourselves. Why is this important to discuss? Because it is important enough to be in the Bible. If God thinks enough of a subject to even mention it, I have to assume it is of enough importance for me to try to understand it.

2 Corinthians 8:9 tells us, "for ye know the grace of our Lord Jesus Christ, that, though he was rich, yet for your sakes he became poor, that ye through his poverty might be rich."

"See there, Pastor! That's just spiritual riches."

"See there, Pastor! I told you He was a poor man."

Strange, isn't it? Those two, completely separate and opposite thoughts, could come out of the same brain? That was "spiritual" riches, and yet not "spiritual" poverty. I wonder if the gold on the streets is "spiritual", too. If it is OK for God to have so much monetary blessing, why is it not OK for His children to enjoy some of the same kind of blessing? If money will ruin one of God's children, is there a possibility the nasty stuff will ruin God, too?

"He was rich." Does that refer to heaven only, or was He wealthy here, too? Let's see if we can arrive at an answer by asking a few questions.

Did Jesus have a treasurer? Yes, Judas the thief.

How many poverty-stricken people that you know either have, or need, a treasurer?

0.

How could a poor man run a ministry that paid all the food and lodging expenses for between twelve and eighty-two men, most of whom were businessmen, presumably accustomed to more than eating out of trash cans and sleeping in the street? He could not accomplish it all and remain poor.

How poor were Jesus' beginnings? He was attended to by kings who brought offerings to Him. Kings don't give gifts based on what they think the recipient is worth—they give based on what they think of themselves. I can't believe that these men would travel for over two years just to get to Jesus, then give him a little pinch of gold dust, a couple of grains of frankincense, and a drop or two of myrrh.

The reality is this: Yes, Jesus was born in a stable. He did not stay in the stable. Yes, His dad was a carpenter. Today, he would be referred to as a building contractor. Considering the way things were done then, Joseph probably had one of the best businesses in the area. He was not a poor little guy that fooled around with wood and hoped to get paid once in a while. Even if Jesus would have been born into the wealthiest family on the whole earth, what He gave up to come here was staggering. All of earth's best was just so much dung by comparison. Both 'poverty' and 'wealth' are relative terms. Relatively speaking, Jesus left the grandeur, position, wealth and glory of Heaven, and when He got here, even the noblest of births in the best of families would have been, by comparison like moving into the basement of a two-holer.

"Oooooh! Pastor! That's gross!!"

No, that's love!

He did it all for us! He did it so that we, through His relative poverty might experience relative riches—spiritual, mental, physical, emotional, financial, social and political. Why are not more Christians wealthy, then? Because so many of God's people are convinced it is Godly to be poor.

"But Pastor, even Jesus said it was hard for a rich man to enter into heaven."

Let's see what Mark10:23-24 says, "And Jesus looked round about, and saith unto his disciples, 'How hardly shall they that have riches enter into the kingdom of God!' And the disciples were astonished at his words. But Jesus answereth again, and saith unto them, 'Children, how hard it is for them that trust in riches to enter into the kingdom of God'."

When Jesus looked around and said "It's tough for a rich person to enter the kingdom of God", His disciples were astonished at His words. Have you ever talked about rich people with a person who is very poor? Their response would certainly not be one of astonishment. They would heartily agree—"Amen, Lord! You tell 'em. All those fat, spoiled, rich babies will just never make it. Tell 'em!" The fact that these men were astonished should be enough to alert us to a different set of facts.

Why were they astonished? Could it possibly be that some of them had money? Could it possibly be that they observed the fact that Jesus had money? If those possibilities are valid, and I think they are, can we assume that the real issue in this passage is not money, but rather trust in money, as Jesus said in His second sentence? Let me repeat: If money would ruin us, or keep us out of heaven, the devil would make sure we had enough of it to choke an elephant! If having money made us bad, the devil would do anything he could to make you very bad. If having money made you bad, why did Jesus have a treasurer? Peter, James, John and Andrew, just to name a few, were businessmen. Did they do it for the money (bad boys), or did they work their hinders off every night catching and cleaning fish, then fixing their nets because it was such great fun??

Jesus explains further in the next three verses (25-27) in the same chapter. "It is easier for a camel (The Lamsa translation says 'rope') to go through the eye of a needle, than for a rich man to enter into the kingdom of God. And they were astonished out of measure, saying among themselves, 'Who then can be saved?' And Jesus looking upon them saith, 'With men it is impossible, but not with God: for with God all things are possible.'" Generally speaking, if I understand what Jesus meant here, wealth can deceive a man to the point that he makes living a Christian life about as tough as threading a needle with a rope and he's already found the needle with the biggest eye! It is tough, but not anywhere near as impossible as we may think—our money neither intimidates nor offends God.

In the back part of my Strong's Concordance, I looked up the various Greek words that are translated "riches." They mean, "fullness of wealth, money and possessions," "valuable bestowment that is useful and needed." So, why am I doing all this talking about wealth and riches? To try to get you to see that our heavenly Father is the blesser, not the curser. In fact, I'd like to show that to you in the Bible.

Galatians 3:13-14 tells us that, "Christ hath redeemed us from the curse of the law, being made a curse for us: for it is written, 'Cursed is everyone that hangeth on a tree: That the blessing of Abraham might come upon the Gentiles through Jesus Christ;' that we might receive the promise of the Spirit through faith."

Because the Law, as passed down through Moses, was a law of the flesh, it needed and had a curse that went along with it, for the purpose of enforcement and motivation. The Law, summarized in the Ten Commandments, is popularly called "the Law of Moses". It is so, only in that it came from God, through Moses to the Hebrew people. It is, in every aspect, the Law of the Covenant God Made with Abraham in the book of Genesis, chapter 15. We are not going to take time now to look at all of that, but I do recommend it as a fascinating study. Suffice it to say at this time, that the Law was the Law of the Covenant, and it carried with it some tremendous blessings and some bone chilling curses—it was and is a law of and for FLESH.

"Christ hath redeemed us from the curse of the law, being made a curse for us." There is an awesome set of curses attached to the Law, and Jesus has already redeemed us from them all. I want you to turn now in your Bible to Deuteronomy 28 and read verses 15-68 very carefully.

This passage contains the capsulized version of the "curse of the law." You noticed as you read it, some really dire curses which all of us hope will never come upon any of us. This list of curses contains sin of all kinds, poverty of every description, sicknesses and diseases of every kind (notice verse 61—it even covers every sickness not mentioned—talk about complete!), theft of your hard-earned goods, unfaithful mates, children going astray, business failure and many other things. Read this passage of scripture very carefully. It is what we have been redeemed from. Think carefully. If these things are a curse, is it possible that they could come from God, who is a Blesser? No! These things "come to pass, if thou wilt NOT hearken unto the voice of the Lord thy God, to observe to do all his commandments and his statutes, which I command thee this day; that all these curses shall come upon thee and overtake thee;" verse 15. Remember that. The curse operates because people do not pay attention to the Word of God. Sounds like a simple case of "Logical Consequences" to me.

Let's go back to Galatians 3:13-14, where it states the reason Christ has redeemed us out from under the curse of the law—"that the blessing of Abraham might come on the Gentiles through Jesus Christ;" In the first 14 verses of Deuteronomy 28, we find the capsulized blessing of the law. Blessings will overtake us in the city, the field, the storehouse and the supply; our children will be both blessed and a blessing, and our enemies will fall before us. Everything we set our hand to will prosper, and we will be a lender instead of a borrower, etc., etc., etc. It all hinges on whether or not we will simply do what the Word of God says to do. If we will, these abundant blessings will come upon us and overtake us. If we will not, He can't help us—the curse will come upon us and overtake us.

Do you understand what it means when the Bible refers to something "coming upon you and overtaking you?" I think I can explain ...

Have you ever been driving down a country road after dark in the summer? There you are, driving along, minding your own business. All of a sudden, you see a rabbit in the middle of the road, running the other way as fast as he can run (which isn't too bad, as running goes). As you get closer, you see him turn his head, first one way, then the other, yet he keeps running straight ahead as fast as he can go. Why does he turn his head from side to side? Because he is aware that something loud and large and probably dangerous is about to (to put it Biblically) "come upon him and overtake him," as it were. He is afraid, and he wants nothing more than to get out of the way. His only real problem is that the light blinds him and he will not run where he cannot see!

He looks back and forth, hoping to be able to see something pretty soon, but he keeps running straight. You, the driver of the car, can slow down (if you can), even swerve to the side to try to miss the rabbit, but the rabbit's blinded-ness will keep him running right in front of you, even if you turn to the side to get away from him. Indeed, if you can't slow enough, or stop, you will, verily, come upon him and overtake him, yea, even unto the flying of much fur, yea, even unto pain and death.

Did the rabbit deserve what he got? I don't know what kind of sinner that particular rabbit was, but there is a better than even chance he didn't. His only problem was that he refused to step out boldly where he couldn't see. The Bible is very clear on this—God expects us to step out on His Word. He won't necessarily show us what we're going to be stepping on when we step. It might look like we're stepping out on nothing at all. We will never know the redemptive power God has available for us until we step out where we cannot see.

I noticed something amazing about this chapter in Deuteronomy. It not only says that the curse will come upon us and overtake us, it says the same thing about the blessing. We need to ask ourselves a question. "Would I rather be run over by a blessing or a curse?" We also need to acknowledge something about blessings. It says they (the blessings) will come upon us, and overtake us. It does not say that we are supposed to pursue them. It is really hard to get run over by something you are chasing. Hmmm.

"But Pastor, I thought I was supposed to want to be blessed." We can want all we want. Just don't pursue the blessings—it messes up our focus. Pursue instead the Word of God and obedience to it—the blessings will find us in their own good time.

One more thing I want to point out before we go on to another aspect of the character and nature of God. You probably noticed in reading through the curse of the law in Deuteronomy 28 that it said, "The Lord will cause" this or that to "come upon you." When I began to understand the character and nature of God, phrases like that really bothered me. I reasoned, "If God is supposed to be Good, Loving, Gracious, Merciful, and all that stuff, how can He, in good conscience, treat people like that?" I was unwilling to ascribe to God the same character shortfalls that beset the Human Race. I believe He is nicer than that. I believe He is God, and therefore incapable of being like us. We, on the other hand, can become like Him. I kept studying until I found an answer to my dilemma.

Verbs.

The English language has only two kinds of verbs. They denote either action or state of being. Whenever a verb is used, it always shows some kind of action or state of being. It may not show who did it, or when, but when the English language uses a verb it is showing direct or indirect cause or state of being. This seems kind of silly to be concentrating on, but I assure you, it is important. You see, the Bible is translated into English out of two major original languages: Hebrew and Greek. The passages that say, "God did" this or that to somebody or other, are almost all found in the Old Testament, which is translated from Hebrew. The Hebrew language, unlike English, has no less than six different kinds of verbs! One of these kinds of verbs is called passive. In these cases in which a passive verb was used in Hebrew, we would more accurately understand it if it had been translated, "The Lord will allow (that is, He cannot stop) this or that," instead of just inserting an English verb, which makes it read, "God did (directly or indirectly) this or that."

"Well, Pastor, I disagree. I don't think you can just pick apart the Bible like that and expect people to believe any of it."

All right. Let's assume that all this "verb" stuff is a bunch of bunk, and let's assume, for the sake of argument that God actually did all that stuff. Did He have a right to do it? Did His doing those things violate His character and nature or did it violate His covenant in any way?

I believe He did have a right to do that under the Old Covenant, and I believe it did not violate His character and His covenant in any way. The Old Covenant was a covenant of flesh, and was enacted on and by the flesh of the Israeli people. It wasn't until Jesus came along that any distinction was made between what a person actually did and what they thought. It was Jesus who brought to their attention that God expected more than just a physical adherence to the Law. Because the Law is designed to control the flesh, and cannot in any way touch the spirit of man, punishments of the flesh are within the realm of the one responsible for the covenant—God Himself, and none other. The bottom line is that God, Old Covenant or New, is a Blesser. It is not just what He does, it is who He is—it is part and parcel of His nature and His character. Without belaboring this point any further, let's go on to the next point.

God is a Rewarder. Genesis 15:1 says that "the word of the Lord came to Abram in a vision, saying, 'Fear not, Abram: I am thy shield, and thy exceeding great reward.'"

Do you notice that God said He was Abram's reward? Which would you rather have, something God could give you, or God Himself? It doesn't take great brilliance to figure out that God, right off the top, offered Abram the very Highest reward that could possibly be offered—God Himself.

The last part of Hebrews 11:6 tells us that God is a "rewarder of them that diligently seek Him." God will always reward the diligent seeker. Even if the seeker doesn't do it right, (which is much of the time) God will be faithful to reward that seeker.

Sometimes I think that we don't know what we need, in reality, and therefore don't know how to go about getting our real needs met. This causes a lot of flailing around in frustration, thinking that God is not answering our prayers, when He is doing His best to get us to just ask the right questions! If you and I will just seek after God in His Word and in prayer, He will reward us. What's the best reward? What do you NEED? Revelation 22:12 reads like this: "And behold, I come quickly; and my reward is with me, to give to every man according as his work shall be."

I thought for years that this verse said that when Jesus comes, He's bringing something with Him to give to me as a reward. It doesn't say that. He said He's coming. Quickly. He also said His reward is with Him. He didn't say His reward would be in the saddlebags on the big white horse, and He would be makin' a list, an' checkin' it twice, etc., etc. Santa Claus He ain't.

Most of the time, we (that is we, not you) Christians are so fleshly that all we can think about is what stuff we are going to get, or what we want. Now, God doesn't have anything against stuff, per se, but He also knows that stuff makes a lousy focus for our attentions. If we can read, we can figure out that God's idea of a good focus for our attentions is Jesus. He said He is our exceeding great reward. He said seek Him, and we'll get rewarded. He said His reward is with Him. Once we can get our focus straight, get our eyes on Jesus, and seek Him rather than Stuff, all the rewards we can stand will be there automatically. Seek Jesus. Get Him, and you've got all the rewards you'll ever be able to handle, in this life or the next.

One more thing about rewards before we go on. It is the nature of a reward to be far greater than anything we could possibly have to do to get it.

For an example, let's say I let my precious dog Poopsy out to do his Poopsy thing on the lawn (preferably somebody else's), and good old Poopsy disappears. I get concerned that maybe Poopsy's sense of direction got messed up by something he smelled, so I call the radio station and offer a reward for the safe return of my precious Poopsy. Down the street, a ways from my house, you are listening to the "Pet Patrol" on the radio, and happen to be looking out your window. There, as big as life, squats Poopsy. Poopsying on your lawn. You go outside and gather up my dog, and call me to come and get him. I come hurrying down the street, greet a blissfully wiggling Poopsy, and hand you a crisp $100 bill. Sweetie, that is not a paycheck, because you didn't work that hard—it is a reward. You did something to earn it, but the size of the reward far outweighs the size of the task you performed in order to get it.

God is our Healer. Although in some circles it is not Theologically Correct to believe this way, the Bible is quite clear that another of the facets of God's nature and character is that He is our healer. I have never figured out what is so great about being sick that people have to come up with a whole branch of theology telling us that's the way God wants it. If that were true, don't you think it would be rather double-minded of Him to say He would heal us?

"Well, Brother, that's just your interpretation."

Let me see if I can write out a few quotes from the Scriptures. No interpretation. No added statements. Just the pure, bald, Word of God, and nothing else. Then we can see if I am interpreting something or just reading it, and choosing to believe what I read.

Exodus 15:26 — "And said, 'If thou wilt diligently hearken to the voice of the Lord thy God, and wilt do that which is right in His sight, and wilt give ear to His commandments, and keep all His statutes, I will put none of these diseases upon thee, which I have brought upon the Egyptians: For I am the Lord that healeth thee.'"

Isaiah 53:5 — "But He was wounded for our transgressions, He was bruised for our iniquities: the chastisement of our peace was upon Him; and with His stripes we are healed."

Psalms 103:2-5 — "Bless the Lord O my soul, and forget not all His benefits: Who forgiveth all thy diseases; Who redeemeth thy life from destruction; who crowneth thee with lovingkindness and tender mercies; who satisfieth thy mouth with good things; so that thy youth is renewed like the eagle's."

Psalms 107:20 — "He sent His word and healed them, and delivered them from their destructions."

Matthew 8:17 — "That it might be fulfilled which was spoken by Esaias the prophet, saying 'Himself took our infirmities, and bare our sicknesses.'"

1 Peter 2:24 — "Who his own self bare our sins in his own body on the tree, that we, being dead to sins, should live unto righteousness: by whose stripes ye were healed."

In the previously quoted verses, there is not one word of interpretation from me. God's Word says, without any help from me at all, that He is the Lord that heals us. It says that His stripes are for our healing. It says that one of the benefits He has for us is to heal all our diseases. It says that He took away our infirmities, and carried our diseases. And if saying it once were not enough, the scripture says again that the stripes He took are for our healing.

"Oh, Come On, John, that's spiritual healing!"

If God is smart enough to say what He means and honest enough to mean what He says, why didn't God say that? According to Scripture, our healing is an accomplished fact, waiting on us. Why do I harp on this? I harp on this because it is an integral part of God's nature, which, if we don't understand it, will stop us from receiving the fullness of God's bounty toward us.

God is our Protector. The last part of God's character and nature I want us to look at (not the last there is by any means, just the last we are going to look at here) is the fact that God is our Protector.

In Genesis 15:1 God tells Abram, "I am thy shield." What is the purpose of a shield? To protect. Especially to protect from things that the person's natural abilities cannot protect against. Skin is a lousy deterrent to the edge of a sword. Ribs are a lousy deterrent to arrows. A shield, of whatever size, makes it's bearer thousands of times safer than he would ever be without it.

It is also interesting to note in this passage that God didn't say He had a shield for Abe, or that Abe didn't need to worry about where the shield was going to come from. He said that He is Abe's shield. It is a better deal to have God Himself as your shield than to borrow one of God's shields, to try to use for yourself. A shield that knows in advance of every arrow that is coming toward us, and can make adjustments accordingly, is lots better than one that we have to maneuver around according to what we can figure out ourselves.

In 2 Samuel 22:1-4 there is a very interesting song that David, King of Israel, sang to the Lord. "And David spake unto the Lord the words of this song in the day that the Lord had delivered him out of the hand of all his enemies, and out of the hand of Saul: And he said, 'The Lord is my rock, and my fortress, and my deliverer; The God of my rock; in Him will I trust: He is my shield, and the horn of my salvation, my high tower, and my refuge, my savior; thou savest me from violence. I will call upon the Lord, who is worthy to be praised: so shall I be saved from mine enemies.'"

Did you hear all the symbolism of protection in that song? David obviously felt very secure in his God, to use such words as "Rock," "Deliverer," "Shield," "Salvation," "High Tower," "Refuge," and "Savior," and he could say, "I trust in thee."

David said again, in Psalms 28:7 that "the Lord is my strength and my shield," and that "my heart trusted in Him." To know that God Himself has promised to be a shield to you is one of the most wonderfully peace-enhancing things you can know. If God's own Word is any good, and it is, He is our protector. He will protect us from whatever it may be that we need to be protected against. We can rest in knowing Him as our shield. He is always on guard to preserve us and help us in every situation. We can let His strength save us—He is much more capable of getting that job done than you and I will ever be.

This rather lengthy look at the character and nature of God has been for a purpose. I want us to understand Who it is we are dealing with in the daily affairs of our life. I want us to think about what it means to "know God" and what it means to "trust the Lord." It is not too much of a big deal to think and believe that God can do something for us, but it is another matter entirely to believe that He will do something for us. The only way we have to make that leap in believing is to understand God's character and nature as they are, not as we have been taught they are by religion. Religion has taught us wrongly, and it has unjustly blamed God for things, for which He is not responsible, just to give an answer that gets the religious off the hook of a hard question.

"Pastor, why did my baby die?"

"Pastor, why can't I seem to get healed of this disease?"

"Pastor, why did this thing happen that has hurt me so badly? I feel that I may never recover from the devastation."

Pastor, Why ... ?

These are only a few of the hard questions that pastors have been faced with over the years. It is easy to shuffle the blame for a hard circumstance off on God, and blame His "higher wisdom" for our inability to understand. It is theologically acceptable to give religious platitudes rather than accepting responsibility or even telling the unvarnished truth.

If we don't know why the baby died, say "I don't know, but God didn't do it." We won't get a big medal for being Answer-man of the Year, but we will at least be telling a grieving parent the truth. Most importantly, we will not be delivering a slap in the face to God's character, by charging Him with something He didn't do.

Why is it so hard for pastors to look at a sick person, who is wondering why they aren't seeming to get an answer to their prayers for healing, and say, "I don't know, but I do know it is not because God wants you sick?"

"Well, you know, Brother, Gawd's ways are higher than our ways. Gawd knows what is best for you."

The inference being sidestepped here is that it's obviously not our fault, and certainly not my fault as the pastor, but maybe "Gawd" has a perfectly good reason for wanting us sick. Surely it is supposed to teach us something. If we really believe that tripe, why aren't we praying for all our friends and family to get cancer, so they, too, can be blessed of "Gawd?"

Because, even on our lamest day, we're not that ignorant, that's why!! Why do we keep putting our brains on "hold" when we think about "Gawd?" I don't think it is a particularly exciting prospect for God, to have to try to fellowship with a crew of purposefully brain-dead "experts." If He's trying to get something across, it is through and with His Word, and by His Spirit, that He is doing it.

What about those people who have hurt us? What about how betrayed we feel? If we have been around religious circles very long, we have undoubtedly heard some kind of sermon about the blessings of betrayal, and how Gawd intends for it to happen to us, so we can become strong through it. Was it a blessing for Jesus? It got Him beaten and killed. I'm not sure He thought of it in terms of being blessed. Have you ever been betrayed? Has someone turned on you, destroyed years of friendship, and torn your heart? Were you blessed? Are you over it yet? Did you get close to God, or did you just hurt until you learned to deal with it? Suffering of any kind does not make the sufferer closer to God. It makes him suffer. Pain of any kind does not make the bearer more spiritual. It makes him hurt. Betrayal does not make the betrayed one strong. It makes him fear people. What are the purposes for betrayal and emotional pain? They are designed to destroy you. Nothing less. So what does God want you to do about it? Forgive the persons responsible, get into the Word for your strength, and GO ON.

"But, Pastor, what about Job?"

four
Job's Problems

I encourage you to read the book of Job in your Bible before you go on in this book. It will help you in seeing what I am going to point out in this chapter. Most people have never read Job because it's rather boring and somewhat hard to follow. Those that have read Job have read with their religious filters firmly in place and their "real world" brain firmly in neutral. This chapter is a study of the book of Job, to find out exactly what happened to him and why, and also to find out who was responsible for what. Sounds like a tall order, but I assure you it is not.

    The first thing I want to point out about good ol' Brother Job is that regardless of God's confession about him, he had "I" trouble. Let me explain. A number of years ago I was doing a study on the book of Job and I began to notice something a bit odd that nobody had ever pointed out to me. I got a red pen and began to circle every time Job himself said, "I," "me," "my," "myself," and "mine." In all, there are 42 chapters in the book of Job and of those 42 chapters, Job himself speaks in just 18 of them. None of the chapters in Job are very long, so I was quite surprised when I began to count up all the words I had circled in red ink. Job talked about HIMSELF, using those five personal pronouns, no less than 700 times. Seven Hundred Times!!!!! Seven hundred, for pity's sake! If a person talked that much about himself while we were listening to him, we would conclude that he was a pretty self-centered guy, wouldn't we? So, why are we so willing to believe that Job was this perfectly wonderful and marvelous man that never did anything wrong and never did have his priorities out of whack?

"But, Pastor! God said that Job was "a perfect and upright man, one that feareth God, and escheweth (really old word that means "hates") evil".

In fact, God said that twice! Exactly, but let's think together for a moment. Think about the last chapter in this book—not the end, but the last one we just read—and think about the nature and character of God. Does God think the best of people? He does if He walks in love, the way He commands that we should do. Does God expect to possess whatever He says? If Creation is any indication, He does. The beginning of Genesis is full of places that say things like, "And God said ... and it was so." That tells me that God doesn't throw words around like we do. God speaks of those things that don't yet exist, as though they were already a reality. Romans 4:17b says "... God, who quickeneth the dead, and calleth those things which be not as though they were." That's how God talks, because His words come to pass!

If that is true, and it is, what would happen to us if God spoke about us the way we do? What if God spoke about Job the way he really was? "Have you considered Job? He likes to think he's my servant, but numbskulls like him are a dime a dozen. He's immature, irreverent, has little respect for the things of God, walks in fear all the time, and gets along pretty well with most kinds of evil. And he's a selfish pig."

If God didn't speak well about Job, and about you and me for that matter, what possible hope would he, or we, ever have of improving in any way? God spoke about Job as though he were the best in all the land, because God was on Job's side and He desired to cause him to overcome, if he ever decided to do so.

"Then why did God send the devil after him the way He did?"

Did God do that? Let's take a Biblical look at Job, letting the

Scripture explain itself, and using our own God-given ability to reason and ask questions.

Job 1:5 says, "And it was so, when the days of their feasting were gone about, that Job sent and sanctified them, and rose up early in the morning, and offered burnt offerings according to the number of them all: For Job said, 'It may be that my sons have sinned and cursed God in their hearts.' Thus did Job continually." Do you see what Job is doing here? He is offering a sin-sacrifice continually and he is doing so on the basis of a maybe. According to the Scriptures, a person is supposed to offer sacrifice for his own sin, when or if he sins! I can't find one single verse that says a man is supposed to offer sacrifice for his grown children's sins, just in case they might have committed them!

Job had apparently reached the place where he had neither faith in his sacrifices nor faith in God; the formality of his religious observances had become the substitute for his faith.

The last part of Romans 14:23 says that "... whatsoever is not of faith, is sin." According to this passage of Scripture, Job was committing sin every time he offered one of those sacrifices for his sons. If my calculator works right, Job sacrificed by bleeding out, then burning whole, ten animals, either goats, sheep or cattle, all males each and every day—that's Three Thousand, Six Hundred and Fifty Crispy Critters a year! Job committed the same sin, over and over and over again (sound familiar?), out of fear, based on a maybe!

Can you see now, that Job was not this wonderful, perfectly Godly fellow who was just minding his own wonderful, perfectly Godly business, with his own wonderful, perfectly Godly family, and his own wonderful, perfectly Godly friends, when God, for reasons Job could not possibly have known, turned him over to Satan, right out of the clear blue, just to prove a point??

Job must have known from the start that all the horrible stuff that was happening to him was somehow connected to his fear, but he still didn't have much of a clue about why his worry (read, "fear") couldn't prevent its happening. In chapter 3, verses 25 and 26, Job is talking about this very thing: "For the thing which I greatly feared is come upon me, and that which I was afraid of is come unto me. I was not in safety, neither had I rest, neither was I quiet; yet trouble came."

Job said, "I was afraid, and it happened anyway. I was really afraid, and it came to me in spite of it. I didn't feel safe, I was restless, and I couldn't keep quiet about it at all, yet trouble showed up anyway. I worried as much as I possibly could about my kids and my goods and my money, but it didn't do a bit of good—trouble came anyway." Isn't it amazing that we are so consistent about treating fear and worry as something that might, this time, actually do some good?

In 2 Timothy 2:25-26, we find something very interesting. "In meekness instructing those that oppose themselves; if God peradventure (antique word meaning "perhaps" or "maybe") will give them repentance to the acknowledging of the truth; and that they may recover themselves out of the snare of the devil, who are taken captive by him at his will." It appears that there are some people who oppose their own best interests. How does one do that? Worry and fear are among the best of ways to destroy your own blessings in life. I think Job qualified as one who opposed himself. What is God's desire for someone who opposes himself? That he repent, and come to acknowledge the truth, and that he recover himself out of the devil's snare.

How did he get there? He was against himself through sin, (fear, in Job's case) and Satan came along and pulled him in whenever he (Satan) was ready—at his will, not necessarily at the will of the snared believer, not at Job's will, and certainly not at God's will. I believe it is safe to say that when a person gets himself out from under the protecting hand of God through unbelief that Satan is free to attack at his (Satan's) will. You get under there by faith, and you stay under there by faith. Only faith's opposite can get you out from under the protecting hand of God

We have already seen in the first five verses, a little bit about Job and what he was doing with his spiritual life. Now let's look at verses 6-8.

"Now there was a day when the sons of God came to present themselves before the Lord, and Satan came also among them." Do we see the distinction made between "the sons of God" (Bible scholars more knowledgeable than I, all agree that this refers to the angels) and Satan? Satan came among them. He was not one of them. Why was Satan there? Obviously, he had a legal right to be there—more on this later in this chapter.

"And the Lord said unto Satan, 'Whence comest thou?'" A lot of people have deduced from the fact that God asked the first question, that God must have been directing Satan's attention to Job, and giving His permission to go attack Job. Not So!! Does God know everything? If you believe that, then you only have a couple of options about this question, and the ones that follow it: either it is a stupid question, or a leading question.

I have a really hard time believing that the God of all Creation, King of Heaven and Earth, and Maker of All that in them is, could ask a dumb question. If, on the other hand, it is a leading question, what kind of leading question is it? Again, we have a couple of choices. Either it is a question designed to get information, or a question designed to let the one being questioned know that information is already possessed by the questioner. Do you think God asks questions because He doesn't know something? No? If we believe that God knows EVERYTHING, we are left with only one conclusion: God is using questions to let Satan know that He knows exactly what's going on, and exactly with whom and exactly where the boundaries have been set. God is not using questions to direct Satan's attention to Job so Satan could say, "OH! Hey! There's one I overlooked! Let's see now ..."

What was Satan's response to God's question? "From going to and fro in the earth and walking up and down in it." The situation brought to mind by this scene from Job took place quite often in my childhood home.

All six of my parent's children slept in the three bedrooms in the upstairs part of the house. I was the youngest, so much of the time, I didn't have any other kids around to distract me from doing what I wanted to do to entertain myself. One of my favorite pastimes was to slip quietly upstairs and jump on the beds. My mother would come to the stairway door and call up, "Johnny! What are you doing up there?" (Hear "Whence comest thou?")

I was quite a bit older before I figured out how she knew I was even up there, much less doing anything. "Nothing, Mom." (Hear, "Going to and from and walking up and down in the earth.")

Then came a response, which at the time completely mystified me. "You wouldn't be jumping on the bed, now, would you?" (Hear, "Have you considered my servant Job ... ") How did she know? Did she really know everything, like she told me she did? Was she just fishing for information? Was this her sly way of suggesting that jumping on the beds might be a fun thing to do and that I should try it as soon as I get some time?

My response was standard. "No, Mom, I just sat down on it (Yeah, from way up in the air). It might have bounced a little when I did that." Poor, dumb Mom. What she didn't know wouldn't hurt me. Heh. Heh.

Finally, the interchange ended with the mystical statement, which has been proof positive for generations that Mothers are Supernatural—"Well, quit it! Beds were not made for jumping!"

I'm sure most of us have had some kind of similar scene enacted during our growing up: those early years when we know full well where the boundaries are, and yet we push against them, only to run full tilt into the very Maker of the Boundaries, and the Setter of the Limits—Dad and Mom.

Can you see the situation in Job? God asks Satan where he has been, and Satan responds, "Oh, nowhere, really. You know, just sort of cruising around, like. Just kinda walking around smelling things, you know. Heh. Heh.

"Have you considered my servant Job, that there is none like him in all the earth, a perfect and upright man, one who respects God and hates evil?" Can you hear God, by asking this question, telling Satan that He knows full well where he has been spending his time and exactly what he has been thinking about?

Verses 9 and 10 tell us that, "Then Satan answered the Lord, and said, 'Doth Job fear God for naught? Hast not Thou made an hedge about him, and about his house, and about all that he hath on every side? Thou hast blessed the work of his hands, and his substance is increased in the land.'" This is not GOD telling Satan all about Job's stuff, and the hedges built up around all of the blessings God had given him! This is SATAN telling God all about it! All God told Satan was what a great guy Job was—He never once mentioned how much stuff Job had, nor how the hedge of his faith protected it all. This is

Satan, proving that he had indeed been spending considerable time working on Job, getting him to tear down his own hedges.

Now look carefully in verse 11, and you'll see Satan trying to talk God into destroying Job and all of his stuff, just to prove whether or not Job would remain faithful, and not curse God. Notice whose idea that was? You will also see, as we read further, that God would not even consider such a thing. Satan said to God, "But put forth thine hand now, and touch all that he hath, and he will curse thee to thy face."

Now, in verse 12, we see God telling Satan that He knows full well that Job has withdrawn his hedges, and that they no longer protect anything but Job himself. "And the Lord said unto Satan, 'Behold, all that he hath is in thy power; only upon himself put not forth thine hand'." God didn't point out to Satan that all of Job's peripheral stuff was placed within Satan's power. He pointed out that He knew what Satan already knew—Job, through fear, has withdrawn his hedges, and now the hedge of faith is around nothing but Job himself.

In Job chapter 1:13-19, we see that all of Job's possessions, including his children, were under the power of Satan, to be taken at Satan's will—God could not stop it at all: "And there was a day when his sons and his daughters were eating and drinking wine in their eldest brother's house: And there came a messenger unto Job, and said, 'The oxen were plowing, and the asses feeding beside them: And the Sabeans fell upon them, and took them away; yea, they have slain the servants with the edge of the sword, and I only am escaped alone to tell thee.' While he was yet speaking, there came also another, and said, 'The fire of God is fallen from heaven, and hath burned up the sheep, and the servants, and consumed them; and I only am escaped alone to tell thee.' While he was yet speaking, there came also another, and said, 'The Chaldeans made out three bands, and fell upon the camels, and have carried them away, yea, and slain the servants with the edge of the sword; and I only am escaped alone to tell thee.' While he was yet speaking, there came also another and said, 'Thy sons and thy daughters were eating and drinking wine in their eldest brother's house: And behold, there came a great wind from the wilderness, and smote the four corners of the house, and it fell upon the young men, and they are dead; and I only am escaped alone to tell thee.'"

Do you hear the depth of the Bad News??? This much tragedy coming upon a person is very hard to comprehend much less deal with. Through what happened to Job, many of us have been led to believe that the only possible explanation for this is that God did it, and that His reasons cannot be understood. This is apparently what Job himself believed at this time. We can infer this from what he said next, in verses 20-21: "Then Job arose, and rent his mantle, and shaved his head, and fell down upon the ground, and worshipped, and said, 'Naked came I out of my mother's womb, and naked shall I return thither; the Lord gave, and the Lord hath taken away, blessed be the name of the Lord.'"

"See there, Pastor? God really did do all that stuff to Job! It says so right there in the Bible!"

First, before we go on, let me make a statement which will probably confuse you, but which I believe I can clear up shortly. Everything in the Bible is true, but not everything the Bible says is the truth.

"That sounds like double-talk to me, but even if it's not, how can that be? You said yourself that everything the Word says is good enough to stake your life on!"

You are absolutely right, I did, and it is. In 2 Timothy, 2:15, it says, "Study to shew thyself approved unto God, a workman that needeth not to be ashamed, rightly dividing the word of truth." When does a workman need to be ashamed? When he doesn't study! When he doesn't rightly divide the word of truth.

So, how does one go about rightly dividing the word of truth? Are there rules that govern such a thing, and if there are, what are they?

Yes, there are rules that govern the study of the Word. No, they are not a kind of mystical, cosmic regulation, without which you will surely go to hell. They are rules of logic and understanding. First, we must know where we are in God's scheme of things. We are living under the New Covenant, ratified by Jesus' blood, sealed and administered by the Holy Spirit. That means the Scriptures that were written for those under the Old Covenant are designed for our instruction and edification, but they are not specifically designed to teach us how to function under the New Covenant. We don't throw the baby out with the bath water. We don't ignore those passages of

Scripture, nor treat them as if they were not valid. Their validity is in teaching us and giving us an example, not in giving us the specifics of our Covenant.

Second, we must study enough to know the balance of Scripture, in the many things it addresses. We must know the character and nature of God—not what somebody told us so they could avoid taking responsibility, but what the Bible actually says. We must know how and why God responds to us as He does under this Covenant.

Third, we must have enough faith in the Author of the Bible to allow the Bible to interpret itself. When we come upon a passage that stumps us, we mustn't be so quick to run to someone else's opinion. We must be patient and let the Holy Spirit teach us through the only instrument He has to teach our spirit—the Word of God. God is really smart. If we give Him a little time and apply some effort to studying out the answer, He can even figure out the things that confuse us!

Everything in the Bible is true, but not everything the Bible says is the truth.

Job said, in verses 21, and 22, "… naked came I out of my mother's womb, and naked shall I return thither: the Lord gave, and the Lord hath taken away; blessed be the name of the Lord.' In all this, Job sinned not, nor charged God foolishly." It is true Job said this. But is this a statement of truth? Is it part of the nature and character of God to give? Absolutely! Is it part of the nature and character of God to take away what He has given? Not at all! God is not a fickle giver. He doesn't give with one hand and take away with the other. God gives—period. But Job said God did it. Why? Because Job believed God did it.

Why did he believe something that was wrong? Probably for the same reason the rest of us do—because he didn't know. Just like the rest of us, Job (and the people around him) filled in the blanks in their ignorance with what they could figure out. God, in His great grace and mercy, does not hold us accountable for what we do not know. Job didn't know about God's nature and character—he had no Bible. In fact he didn't even have the Law of Moses. "In all this Job sinned not, nor charged God foolishly." Why? Because Romans 7:8b, says "… for without the Law, sin was dead …" Job didn't know! He had no revelation of Satan and very little revelation of God.

For the most part, Job 1:7-8 reads exactly like Job 2:2-3. As we discussed earlier, we can see God asking 'leading' questions of the devil, and speaking forth His wonderful confession concerning His servant Job. In chapter 2, we can see God asking Satan the very same question he asked him the first time he came before Him, "From whence comest thou?" Why is He asking this question? Why ask it again? Because the situation had not changed. Satan gave Him the same run-around answer, "From going to and fro in the earth, and from walking up and down in it." God used the same "leading question" format to let Satan know the first time that He knew exactly what was going on and that He would be keeping a close eye on the boundaries Job had set.

In the last part of Job 2:3, we see that God departed from saying exactly the same thing He had said before. "... and still he holdeth fast his integrity, although thou movedst me against him, to destroy him without cause." God didn't do it, but Satan tried to get Him to do it. God said that which came upon Job was "destruction", and that it came upon him "without cause." God did not consider Job's self-centeredness and fear a worthwhile cause for his destruction, no matter who was doing the destroying!

In Job 2:6, God tells Satan, "Behold, he is in thy hand, but save his life." For years, Bible teachers have looked at this statement and assumed that God was giving His permission for Satan to beat the stuffing out of Job. Not so. All God is doing here is telling Satan specifically where the boundaries are which Job has set and that he'd better not go past them.

Do you remember back to Job 1:12, in which God told Satan the first time what the boundaries were? He told Satan, "... only upon himself put not forth thine hand." Literally everything Job had, and everything his family had, had been gained by Job using his faith for the blessing of God. Then he started that nasty "what if" spiral that caused his faith to retreat until it was protecting nothing but Job's own person, and nothing else. The scripture says, "... upon himself ..." was the limit to which Job's faith had withdrawn. Now go to Job 2:6, in which God says, "... save his life ..." After all of Job's blessings, and family and possessions had been taken away from him, he withdrew his faith even further until it no longer protected his body, it was just good enough to keep him alive, and no more. God did not give Satan permission to go hurt Job. He was only telling Satan what Satan already knew—where the boundaries are, and not to go beyond them.

"But Pastor! I don't get it! Why did God keep telling Satan about those boundaries?"

Read Ezekiel 28, verses 12-19. We can see that Satan, at one time, tried to take over the very throne of God, and for his efforts, was kicked out of heaven. Satan is as much an illegal bully as the Mafia ever hoped to be, and like all bullies, he constantly pushes in where he has no right to be. God is not the kind of guy that puts up with a bunch of monkey business on His watch. If we choose to, that's up to us. God simply told Satan, "I know the degree to which Job's faith has retreated, and I want you to know I know."

The middle parts of the book of Job, though interesting, do not hold enough of the issues we need to look at for the purpose of discussing the question, "What about Job's problems?" I do encourage you to read the whole book, as there is much there to learn, even though we are not stopping there now.

As we approach the end of the book of Job, we see things beginning to turn around for him. Why? Let's look.

Job 38:1 — "Then the Lord answered Job ..." God spoke!!! The Word of God was given, concerning His nature, character, and power! What happens when someone hears the Word of God? Romans 10:17 says "So then, faith cometh by hearing and hearing by the Word of God." What happens when someone hears the Word of God? Faith Happens! After Job heard the Word of God and faith came, Job was the only one around there God would listen to. In Job 42:8, God said to Job's "friends" that they needed to go and get Job to sacrifice for them, because "... him will I accept ..." because "... ye have not spoken of me the thing which is right, like my servant Job ..." Job heard the Word of God, which is the only thing that brings faith to the heart of a person; after that, Job's was the only prayer to which God would listen, and Job's the only sacrifice He would accept.

As we can see in Job 42:7-8, Job's friends, God said, "... have not spoken of me the thing which is right." God is the one who said they didn't speak right about Him. In fact, when the young one, Elihu, had finished speaking, God said, in Job 38:2, "Who is this that darkens counsel without knowledge?" That sounds like a really classy way of asking, "Why do they let someone that ignorant have the microphone?"

What did they say that God might object to someone's saying about Him? (Once again, notice: God was not objecting to anything they said about Job, just to what these "friends" had said about God!)

In Job 4:9, Eliphaz explains that Job must not be as righteous as everyone has been thinking he is, so Job had better watch out because God gets really angry about people trying to be more righteous than they actually are—in fact, "By the blast of God they perish, and by the breath of His nostrils are consumed." In fact, in that same chapter, verses 14-21, Eliphaz claims to have had a vision and a supernatural visitation, to give a greater credibility to his assessment of Job's problems. He said God did it!!

In Job 8, Bildad speaks, angrily telling Job that God has destroyed Job's children because they were sinners, and that Job's life is a mess because he is a sinner, too.

In Job 11, Zophar accuses Job of some deep, dark sin, and gives that as the obvious reason why God is punishing him. All three of these guys said God did it!!, then Elihu, in chapters 32-37 (a rather long winded sort) comes along and tells them he has waited this long to speak because he has such great respect for their age and maturity, but that he can hold back no longer. He said God did it!! After Elihu was finished rambling on, God said to Job (38:2, poetic license liberally applied) "Who is that runt?"

At long last, God begins to speak. Notice, He did not speak to those who already thought they had all the answers. He only spoke to the one guy who was absolutely certain he needed answers.

In chapter 42:10, the mess Job was in was called "captivity". "And the Lord turned again the captivity of Job, when he prayed for his friends: also the Lord gave him twice as much as he had before." It says in Psalms 126:1 & 4, that God is the one who will "turn again (that Hebrew word means 'release') our captivity." Throughout the book of Judges, God's people went into "captivity" over and over, but, each time, it was God who released them from their captivity by His grace and power.

Remember the "If-God-Says-Something-Once- ..." Principle? The fact that God releases His people from captivity is spoken of in the scriptures no less than 32 times!! It was the Lord who released Job from his captivity, and it was the Lord who gave him twice as much as he had before (and he was "the greatest of all the men of the east" (1:3) before all this happened!).

"Pray for me, Pastor. I'm going through a "Job Experience" right now. Me and Ol' Job, we're just alike."

Hold on a minute, and I can explain to you why a "Job Experience" is not possible for anyone today. Yes, I know that when you are at your lowest, and your circumstances are at their most miserable, that it feels pretty good to think that you may be going through something "Biblical" like that. That is only another lie, to keep us from standing up for ourselves, and getting that mess off our back! Let's look at the Word, and see WHY a "Job Experience" is impossible today.

Job 1:6 and 2:1 both say "... there was a day when the sons of God came to present themselves before the Lord, and Satan came also among them ..." Bible scholars who are much more learned than I agree that the term 'sons of God" is a reference to the angels of God. The angels came to present themselves before the Lord, and "satan came also among them", which tells us that nobody there needed to be very bright to figure out that Satan was not "one of the guys". If there was a day when the sons of the great boxer, George Foreman, came to present themselves before the Champ, and I also came among them, nobody would have to be very bright to figure out that I'm not "one of the guys". I look just as human as the sons do, but you can tell I'm not one of George's!

Satan came and went freely before the throne of God. The fact that he came and went freely, tells us that he had a right to do so. How did he get the right to access the courts of Heaven? When God created Mankind, they were given great authority in heaven and earth. Authority in the earth includes everything earthly. Authority in heaven includes everything up to, but not including, the very throne of God itself (God keeps some things inviolate). God gave all that authority to Adam, and Adam gave it all to Satan when he took the fruit of the tree of the knowledge of good and evil. When Adam fell for Satan's lie, all the authority God had invested in him was usurped by Satan. Then, Praise God, Jesus came. Jesus came to earth and went to the pit of hell to take all that authority back, only to turn right around and give it back to mankind through the Church. However, at the time of Job Satan had a right to come and go throughout all of Heaven, before the very throne of God itself. Do you need some New Testament proof for all this? Read Hebrews 9:23.

"It was therefore necessary that the patterns of things in the heavens should be purified with these; but the heavenly things themselves, with better sacrifices than these." Read it all. That whole chapter is talking about the utensils of earthly worship, and in explaining about those things, the author of the book of Hebrews explains about the actual heavenly utensils of worship, from which the earthly utensils of worship were patterned. Since Jesus had to purify "the heavenly things themselves," with "better sacrifices" we can infer that those "heavenly things" must have needed to be purified, and that a sacrifice of earthly significance wouldn't have been good enough to do the job. If the heavenly utensils of worship had not been defiled (after all, they were made perfect, and never touched by unholy hands until Satan "came and went" before the throne of God) they would not have needed to be purified. Satan was given the right to go before God, by usurping Adams rights and authority. At that time then, he was able to go before God and accuse the people of God, right before His face. There came a time, however, when that became impossible. Let's read Revelation 12:7-10.

"And there was a war in heaven: Michael and his angels fought gainst the dragon; and the dragon fought, and his angels, and prevailed not; neither was their place found any more in heaven. And the great dragon was cast out, that old serpent, called the Devil, and Satan, which deceiveth the whole world: he was cast out into the earth, and his angels were cast out with him. And I heard a loud voice saying in heaven, 'Now is come salvation, and strength, and the kingdom of our God, and the power of His Christ: for the accuser of our brethren is cast down, which accused them before our God day and night.'"

Notice!! "neither was their place found any more in heaven". When the angels of Michael and the angels of the Devil fought, the devil and his crew were thrown out of heaven. Mike and Group did such a thorough job of booting Satan's bootie out of there, that there was no longer any "place" found where any of them could be.

Notice!! "Now is come salvation". When did salvation "come"? Was it when God decided to send Jesus? Not possible! That was "before the foundations of the world". Was it when Jesus was born? Not possible! That was the beginning of the earthly part of the enactment of the plan of God. Was it when Jesus hung on the cross? Not possible! That was the end of the earthly part of the enactment of the plan. Was it when Jesus went to hell? Not possible! That was the beginning of the spiritual part of the enactment of the plan. Was it when Jesus took a drop of His own blood to the "heavenly place of worship and sat down at the right hand of the Father? YYYYEEESSS!!! That moment was when "now" began, and from that moment, Satan could no longer gain direct access to the presence of God.

Notice!! The end of verse 10, where it says "... the accuser of our brethren is cast down, which accused them before our God day and night." Do you see the word "accused?" The "ed" on the end of that word denotes past tense. In the common vernacular, that means he "usta did" "accuse our brethren before our God day and night". That means he did, at one time, accuse the brethren before God day and night, but he does so no longer!

Is he still "the accuser of the brethren"? Yes.

Does he still "accuse our brethren before our God day and night"? No. The closest Satan can get to God is to get to us!!! He still accuses our brethren day and night, but his days and nights are spent accusing us to each other.

He is a destroyer, and he wishes above all else to destroy God. Satan can't do that, so he works to destroy those whom God loves and prizes above all else—the Body of Christ. If we are willing to believe the devil's accusation about another Christian, thinking we are right, we will use our blood-purchased authority to destroy that believer, and in so doing we will destroy ourselves. Church, we already have a devil to deal with, and he surely doesn't need our help in condemning and destroying the Body of Christ.

Get it!! God did not save any of us to be theologically accurate, so we could fix the Body of Christ. He did save us and give us all a command to walk in love.

Here is a pretty good "check-up" — we can't demand that we are "right" (which, by default, means that somebody else is "wrong"), and walk in love at the same time. If somebody is trying to be the doctrinal or prophetic plumb-line for the Church, it is a near total certainty they are not walking in love. Have you checked up on yourself? How are you walking? Can anybody else tell whose side you are on?

five
Paul's Thorn

Many members of the Body of Christ are convinced that Paul's Thorn" was a physical malady that God gave Paul to keep him from being exalted (most people read that word and hear "prideful"). It is true that the thorn was given to keep him from being exalted "above measure", but it was not given to him by God nor was God the one doing the "measuring". 2 Corinthians 12:1-10.

We can see in this passage that Paul did not want to brag on himself. "... yet of myself I will not glory, but in mine infirmities." Paul had learned enough discipline to refuse to promote himself and his accomplishments. In 2 Corinthians 12:1-4, we see that the only thing Paul wanted to do was share with people what God had revealed to him, but he was so circumspect about it as to consider it "unlawful" to talk about it too much. This is not the attitude of a man with an ego problem.

By the way, where do "revelations" come from? There is only one place—the Word of God. In fact, Wisdom, which is the Word of God, speaks in Proverbs 4:8, telling us that if we will "exalt her" (that is, wisdom/the Word), she will "exalt" (or promote) us. So, we can see clearly that Paul, who was the world's foremost Exalter of the Word, got himself exalted by default.

In 2 Corinthians 12:6, Paul said. "For though I would desire to glory (I'd love to toot my own horn, y'all.), I shall not be a fool (I ain't stoopid, hey.); for I will say the truth. Jesus said in John 17:17, "... thy word is truth." You see, Paul knew he did not have to toot his own horn. He knew that if he would just exalt the Word, the Word itself would lift him up high enough for everyone to see. All Paul needed to do was speak the Word (truth).

In verse 7, we see that Paul did indeed receive an "abundance of revelations" and they did "exalt" him. However, somebody seemed to have a "measure" on him—a measure on how much "exaltation" was "too much". Who do you think doesn't want a believer to rise up too high? Is it God? But He is the one that gave the revelations that exalted Paul! If God were actually concerned about Paul's being unable to handle being exalted, do you honestly think He would have trusted him with all of that to start with? I have to believe God is smarter than that! As well, I have to believe He is more mature than that!

The only one who would benefit from Paul's not being exalted is Satan. He could not stop the revelations from coming to Paul because revelations come from the Word of God and Satan cannot stop anyone from getting into the Word. God would get more benefit and glory from a man full of the Word being lifted up higher and higher, than He would get out of a man full of the Word being limited and eventually flattened! Satan knows that the only way a revelation can be made ineffective is for the person who has received it to act as if that revelation were not true.

Satan doesn't care if you talk as if the revelation you have received is true, or even pray as if it is true, so long as you don't live and make decisions as if it is true. Once you conduct your life and make your decisions as if the thing God revealed to you is true, Satan is absolutely powerless to hinder you, much less stop you.

In the last half of verse 7, we see that Paul calls the "messenger of Satan" a "thorn" in his "flesh, sent to buffet" him. Let's take a look at each of these words and phrases in an effort to understand exactly what is being said.

The Greek word that is translated "messenger" is the word "angelos" (look familiar?). It is literally translated "messenger" but in many places in the Scriptures, it is transliterated as "angel." Virtually all Bible scholars agree that the phrase "messenger of Satan", or "angel of Satan", refers only to a demonic entity.

I have found not one place in the Scripture where God has been so personally inadequate that He needs to use a bullying demon to work His will in the Body of Christ. If I, as a human father, hired a neighborhood bully to beat up and terrorize my children, so they would learn a lesson of some sort, I would be arrested for child abuse—it is illegal!! Think about it! How did we get so twisted as to think it is OK for God to do something it is illegal for the average human being to do?

Are we mere mortals held to a higher standard of behavior than God is?

The word "flesh" is the Greek word "sarx". In a few of the verses in which "sarx" is translated "flesh", it is obvious by the context that it is referring to the physical body. In the largest majority of the verses in which "sarx" is translated "flesh", the context demands "the carnal mind" as the appropriate definition. Romans 8:7-8 says "Because the carnal mind is enmity against God: for it is not subject to the laws of God, neither indeed can be: So then they that are in the flesh "sarx" cannot please God." If this reference were to the physical body, the only way we would have of pleasing God would be to die! If God could only be pleased by the death of His people, the most spiritual thing we could do is to kill as many of God's people as possible. Obviously that is not what God wants (it is against the law), so in this reference, as in most other references in scripture, "the flesh" is referring to our "carnal" or "unrenewed" mind

What is referred to as a "thorn" in the Scriptures?

Numbers 33:55 says, "But if ye will not drive out the inhabitants of the land from before you; then it shall come to pass, that those which ye let remain of them shall be pricks in your eyes, and thorns in your sides, and shall vex you in the land wherein ye dwell."

Joshua 23:13 says, "Know for a certainty that the Lord your God will no more drive out any of these nations from before you; but they shall be snares and traps unto you, and scourges in your sides, and thorns in your eyes, until ye perish from off this good land which the Lord your God hath given you."

In both of these passages of Scripture we see some personages or personalities being likened to a "thorn". In both of these instances God told Moses and Joshua how to get rid of their "thorn"—drive them out in the Name of the Lord. Did you notice in these two passages of Scripture that God is not the one who sent the thorn? Did you notice that God did not give the thorn permission to wipe out God's people? All God said was, "Either you kick them out of your land, or this is going to happen to you, and you won't like it." (loose translation).

One of the things God called Paul to reveal to him, and through him to reveal to the Body of Christ, is the Authority of the Believer and the power of the name of Jesus.

2 Corinthians 11:23-27 enumerates a long list of things Paul went through as he went about preaching the gospel: He was in labors more abundant, he took stripes above measure, he was in prisons more frequently and faced death often. Five times he received the 39 stripes that Jesus took. Three times he was beaten with rods (a peculiar form of punishment in which a person was locked in stocks with his feet up in the air, and his feet were then beaten with metal rods until every bone below the ankles was broken), and he was shipwrecked three times as well. He was stoned (they used big, jagged rocks and did not stop throwing them as hard as they could until the person being stoned was dead). He was adrift in the ocean for a night and a day, treading water. He took journeys often. He experienced danger in water, danger from robbers, danger from his own countrymen, danger from the heathen, danger in the city, danger in the wilderness, danger in the sea and he was in danger among false brethren. He was in weariness, painfulness and watching often. He was cold and naked, hungry and thirsty, and he fasted often.

Verse 28 goes on to say that, balanced against this whole list was the one thing which "cometh upon me daily" which is the "care" of all the churches. The Greek word translated "care" is the word "merimna". In Mark 4:18-19, Jesus calls care "merimna" a "thorn" which is designed to make the Word of God unfruitful or ineffective. In 2 Corinthians 12:7, we see that this demon was "buffeting" (the Greek word means to pummel, as a boxer, or to beat thoroughly) his carnal (unrenewed) mind so consistently that he could not relax and move on in the Spirit. Paul became convinced that it must be his job to WORRY about the well being of all the churches he had started, and left in the hands of inexperienced leaders.

2 Corinthians 12:8,9 says "For this thing (the messenger of Satan, the thorn) I besought (begged) the Lord thrice (three times) that it might depart from me. And He said unto me 'My grace is sufficient for thee: for my strength is made perfect in weakness." Most gladly therefore will I rather glory in my infirmities, that the power of Christ

may rest upon me."

Read that again. Did God say, "No, Paul, you can keep this devil, it will make you strong"? No, He did not say that nor imply it in any way!! Let's address a couple more questions as we come to an answer about what God really said in these verses.

First question: To what revelation did God call Paul? Paul himself said in 1 Corinthians 3:10, "I lay a good foundation of the grace of God as it was given to me." The word "grace" is found 97 times in the writings of Paul and only 31 times in the entire remainder of the New Testament. The facts of our Identification with Christ, evidenced by phrases like "in Him," "in Christ," "by whom," "in whom," "by Christ Jesus," and so forth, are found almost exclusively in the writings of Paul. It is the knowledge of Grace, our identification with Christ, and His identification with us, that both proves and works the Authority of the Believer.

Second question: Why did God refuse to answer Paul's prayer to get the devil off his back? According to 2 Corinthians12: 8, Paul prayed three times, in an effort to get God to make this devil go away. Each time he begged God to make the devil go away, God said to him, "My grace is sufficient for thee." The Greek word translated "grace" means "gift" or "favor". God was telling him that the gift of grace that God had given to him would do the job for him. Paul missed the answer to his prayer.

For the purpose of illustration, let's say a man has been teaching his wife how to shoot his .22 rifle. They have been practicing and her skills are improving. One day she comes running in to where he is, in a panic, shouting that there is a snake in the back yard. Instead of jumping up, running out and killing that snake, like the Knight in Shining Armor that he is (and that he is supposed to be), he tells her, "My .22 is sufficient for thee." I can assure you that is not what she wants to hear right then, and that she will continue her entreaties. If he remains firm in his belief in her, and in her abilities to use his "grace gun", she will eventually go outside with the gun, and shoot the snake with the gun. God believes in you, and in your ability to use His "grace gun" to go shoot the serpent for yourself.

Remember that the revelation for which Paul was called was "grace", the "authority of the believer", and "who we are in Christ".

With those things in mind let's look at a few things that are important to any believer's use of God's "grace gun".

Ephesians 1:21-23 says that we are His Body, and that "all things" are "under his feet." Your left eyebrow is a part of your body. If there is something under your feet, that something is also under your left eyebrow—you and the rest of the Body, including the head, are connected!!!

James 4:7 says, "Submit yourself therefore unto God, resist the devil, and he will flee from you." Hmmm. "Resist the devil." If you were to diagram that sentence, you would see that the subject of the sentence is an understood "you"—you resist the devil. Notice, it doesn't say "whine, and God will chase the devil away for you, because you are driving Him crazy." It says, "you resist the devil, and he will flee from you!! It is a no-brainer to believe that the devil might run away from Almighty God. What we need to catch is this: If we act in faith on the Word of God, and if we speak that Word boldly, the devil will run away from us us us us US! Of course the devil is running away because of an irresistible power that does not come from us, and of course he is running away because of the inherent authority of God based in His Word—who cares?? Our Itch For Theological Accuracy makes us so nit picky that we end up talking ourselves out of resisting the devil and taking authority over him the way we are supposed to do, and he ends up not running anywhere. Get A Grip, Church! It makes no difference that the devil obeys you even though you don't deserve the grace you walk in—he obeys you.

Mark 16:17 — "These signs follow them that believe" (Notice it does not say that them that believe are supposed to follow signs from one good meeting to another.), "... in my name, they shall cast out devils ..." (Notice, this does not say that those who believe will pray, and God will get rid of the devil for them)—they cast out the devils themselves.

In Ephesians 4:27 it says, "Neither give place to the devil ..." Again, the subject of the sentence is the understood "You". So it says, "Hey, You! Do not give any place to the devil." Since you and the rest of the believers of the world are in charge of controlling the devil's activities, it seems to me to be an intelligent thing to learn as much as possible about how that's done.

Ephesians 6:11 says, "(You) Put on the whole armor of God, that you may be able to stand against the trickery of the devil." Did you notice this passage of Scripture does not say "Put on the whole armor of God, so that the armor will be able to stand against the trickery of the devil"? The bottom line is simple: God will not do for us what He has given us both the power and the authority to do for ourselves—He believes in us!

In 2 Corinthians 12:9, God spoke two significant things to Paul, and Paul said one thing in response to it.

First, God said, "My grace is sufficient for thee." Paul's revelation of the power and efficiency of the grace of God should have been enough to tell him, and for that matter, me, how to get the devil off his own back.

Second, God said, "My strength is made perfect in weakness". The Greek word translated "strength" is the word "dunamis," which means "explosive, or miraculous power". This word is the root word of our word "dynamite". The Greek word translated "perfect" does not mean "flawless," but rather it means "mature, or full of ability." The Greek word translated "weakness" means "strengthlessness."

Then Paul said, "most gladly therefore will I rather glory in my infirmities ..." The Greek word translated "glory" means "to boast or rejoice," and the Greek word translated "infirmities" means "weaknesses."

God said to Paul, "My grace is enough for you, because My miraculous power is filled with ability, and because you are too weak to do anything on your own." Paul said, "Because that's true, I rejoice in my lack of strength, so your power may freely rest on me."

Notice that in all the definitions of the words translated "infirmity" and "weakness" I've been discussing in the original Greek text, there is not one sickness or physical ailment mentioned. Paul knew and rejoiced in the fact that his own personal weakness (lack of strength) was just another opportunity for God to show Himself strong in a yielded life.

Still not satisfied that Paul's affliction did not come from God and that God did not produce his infirmity (or yours or anyone else's), either directly or by permission? The next chapter is for you.

six
What is an Infirmity?

First, let's start off by looking at some Hebrew and Greek definitions for the words translated "infirmity." There are four Hebrew words translated "infirmity." They mean, "as if menstruating," "to be rubbed or worn," "weak," "weak, as a woman in travail." There are five Greek words translated "infirmity." They mean, "weakness," "feebleness," "strengthless," "impotent," "disability." With these definitions in mind let's look at what the Scriptures say about "infirmities."

Luke 8:2 and 13:11 are similar in their use of some words. In both of these verses, we see the phrase "spirit of infirmity" in direct relation to physical sickness or pain. In some cases of physical sickness or pain, Jesus believed He was dealing with a demon. Obviously, that is not true of every instance or physical sickness or pain, but that is the only time in Scripture the word "infirmity" is used in connection with a physical sickness of pain.

Sometimes an infirmity is of the "flesh". Do you remember the Greek word "sarx", which has to do with our unrenewed, or carnal, mind? Romans 6:19 says, "I speak after the manner of men because of the infirmity of your flesh" This cannot be referring to a sickness or physical ailment because we do not have to speak differently to a sick or hurt person, but we do have to speak differently to someone whose carnality gets in the way of his understanding.

Galatians 4:13 says, "You know how through infirmity of the flesh 'sarx' I preached the gospel unto you at the first." Paul is saying that when he first began to preach the gospel there was something about his carnality that he had to battle through to get the job done. Verse 14 goes on to say that the people received him and the Word of God well, in spite of it.

Matthew 8:17 says, "That it might be fulfilled which was spoken by Esaias (Old English for Isaiah) the prophet, saying 'Himself took our infirmities and bare our sicknesses.'" Jesus took upon Himself on the cross our infirmities and our sicknesses. Do you see the distinction made between sickness and infirmity? Why would Jesus do such a thing? So He would be weaker? No! So we could be strong. Everything Jesus did, He did for us!!

In His earth-walk, Jesus healed sicknesses and infirmities of many different kinds—those that were caused by demons and those which were not. Luke 5:15 says that "… great multitudes came together to hear; and to be healed by Him of their infirmities." Luke 7:21 says that Jesus "… cured many of their infirmities …" In Luke 8:2, we see ministering to Jesus " … certain women which had been healed of evil spirits and infirmities." In John 5:5-9, we see Jesus healing a man incapacitated by an infirmity he had had for 38 years. All these passages, though different from one another, are clear in one central respect—they each talk about people being healed of their infirmities.

In 2 Corinthians 11:30, and 12:5, 9, 10, we see Paul rejoicing in his weaknesses. Romans 8:26 says "Likewise the Spirit also helpeth our infirmities …" Because of the help of the Holy Spirit, we are not to allow any sort of infirmity to slow us down, but rather we are to look upon them as opportunities to overcome! Our attitude will make all the difference in whether or not we actually do overcome.

It is our great blessing that "… we have not an high priest which cannot be touched by the feeling of our infirmities, but was in all points, tempted like as we are, yet without sin." (Hebrews 4:15) How wonderful for us to know that Jesus knows how we feel when our weaknesses get the best of us.

However, Jesus, like any other source of help we may turn to, is only as efficient and effective, as we will allow Him to be. Whenever we take back our burdens and demand to be our own answer, all the power and authority God has at His disposal will simply lie at our feet, inert and useless. If on the other hand we take advantage of Jesus' help in dealing with our weaknesses, we will be able, not only to overcome those weaknesses, but able also to help someone else as well.

It says in Romans 15:1, "We then that are strong ought to bear the infirmities of the weak, and not to please ourselves." We are expected to help others with their infirmities as soon as we get strong enough to overcome our own. We are a family, and we need each other!!

seven
What is an Affliction?

Because I believe it is helpful in gaining an understanding, I want to look at the various definitions of the words in the original languages that are translated "afflict," or "affliction." In Hebrew there are 16 of them, they mean: *pressure, cause to anguish, grief, cause to melt away in fear, crushed, oppressed, to vex, to spoil by breaking in pieces, to bind up and squeeze, depress, to bring into contempt, depressed in mind or circumstances, lowly, poor, to be an enemy to,* and *to make worth nothing.*

In Greek, there are 9 words translated "afflict" or "affliction'. They mean, *hardship, suffering, pain or maltreatment, suffer exasperation, confound or confuse, stir up, be wretched, to crowd or put pressure upon, anguish* and *persecution.*

Keep these shades of meaning in mind as we read the next few verses from the Word. As we look at Scripture to see what God has to say about "affliction" let's try to answer a couple of simple questions.

The first question is, "Does God do it?"

In Psalms 44:2, David said to God, "How thou didst drive out the heathen with thy hand, and plantedst them, how thou didst afflict the people, and cast them out." Here we see it very clearly—yes! God does do it—to His enemies, through His people. Keep in mind that under the New Covenant, God's enemies are not human and neither are ours. God very clearly does not afflict His people. He did it through the hand of His people to their enemies.

God has always made a way for His people to afflict their enemies. In this dispensation of grace we must be aware that, unlike the Old Covenant, none of our enemies are people. Also keep in mind that if we feel that God is afflicting us, we have assumed that we are somehow His enemy. Bad Assumption.

Ruth 1:21 — "I went out full, and the Lord hath brought me home again empty: why then call ye me Naomi, seeing the Lord hath testified against me and the Almighty hath afflicted me?" Naomi certainly was positive in her assessment of her situation, wasn't she? She felt as if she had been devastated, and the devastation was so huge and so complete that it must have come from God! She was so filled with woe! Her feelings of emptiness were so overwhelming that she completely overlooked Ruth. Ruth, who was out in the fields and forests making sure Naomi had something to eat and going to the well every day to make sure she had something to drink and a way to be clean. She was not empty, she just felt empty. God hadn't done it to her, she just felt as though He had.

Isaiah 53:4 says, "We esteemed (which means "thought") him smitten of God, and afflicted." This is a prophecy about Jesus, and his time on the cross. The prophet is speaking from the vantage point of the people who would be surrounding Jesus as He hung there. Those people thought God was doing all that horrible stuff to Jesus. Have you ever noticed in your life that things are different than the way you think they are? I suppose the people in Bible times were about the same as you and me, huh?

God said, in Zephaniah 3:19, "I will undo all that afflict thee." If God were the one to do, or even to will or to allow the afflicting of us, and if this verse is true, then God has just promised to undo himself. The Hebrew word translated "undo" means "the absolute negative of 'Make, Do, Become, or Finish.'" We see by this verse that God takes it very seriously and very personally when someone afflicts His people. He does not like it and He has vowed to do something about it.

2 Samuel 22:28 and Psalms 18:27 both say the same thing: "The afflicted people thou wilt save." God has promised to save us when we are afflicted. If He were the one doing the afflicting, or willing

or allowing us to be afflicted He would have to save us from Himself. Body of Christ, what kind of schizophrenic nut case do we think our Heavenly Father to be?

Proverbs 15:15 tells us that "... all the days of the afflicted are evil." Remember earlier when we discussed the fact that God is Good in the widest sense and application of the term? It is still true. Affliction brings evil to the days of the afflicted one, so it is impossible for that affliction to come from God!

"But, Pastor! God is testing me and teaching me through this affliction!"

Remember James 1:13? It says "Let no man say when he is tempted (the Greek word means "put to the test") I am tempted (tested) of God: for God cannot be tempted (tested) with evil, neither tempteth (tests) he any man." Even if it looks like it must be God doing this to you, or feels like it must be God doing this to you—don't say it. (Let no man say.) It is not God doing this evil thing to you no matter how it feels. God is good and He doesn't have any evil to give away.

Isaiah 49:13-16 tells us that God will comfort His people, and have mercy on those who are afflicted. If God is the giver of the affliction, what kind of goof ball would He have to be to turn around and make a promise of deliverance to comfort those He has just nailed? That "slap and pet" behavior is the classic behavior pattern of an abuser! I absolutely cannot believe that my Heavenly Father is an abuser. If you believe that, to whom do you turn for relief? Could that dilemma have some bearing on the reason so many members of the Body of Christ are addicted to so many things?

Not only does this passage tell us that God has mercy on and comforts those who are afflicted, it tells us that He treats them better than a suckling child! Newborn children are not treated badly! If they should happen to make a mess (and they do), nobody expects them to feel sorry for doing it, much less clean up after themselves. The only thing expected of suckling children is suckling, sleeping, filling diapers, burping and growth. How is it that we, as Christians, can see that someone is a new baby in the Lord, and we expect them to jump up, clean up their own messes, and go to work?

2 Kings 14:26-27 says that the Lord saw the affliction of Israel and saved them. The Scripture is incredibly clear! How could we

become so twisted in our thinking that we could accept so naturally the idea that God could somehow get some kind of glory, or worse yet, pleasure, out of His people being afflicted?? If God somehow thought your affliction was a good deal, or good for you, why would He offer to save you? Nobody is ignorant enough to save someone from something that's good for them.

So, we have established the fact that affliction does not come from God, but, at the same time, we are all aware that afflictions do come. The next logical question then, is "Why?"

Why does affliction come upon us? Let's read again Mark 4:14-20. "The sower soweth the word. And these are they by the way side where the word is sown; but when they have heard, Satan cometh immediately, and taketh away the word that was sown in their hearts. And these are they likewise which are sown on stony ground; who, when they have heard the word, immediately receive it with gladness; And have no root in themselves, and so endure but for a time: afterward, when affliction or persecution ariseth for the word's sake, immediately they are offended. And these are they which are sown among thorns; such as hear the word, And the cares of this world, and the deceitfulness of riches, and the lusts of other things entering in, choke the word, and it becometh unfruitful. And these are they which are sown on good ground; such as hear the word, and receive it, and bring forth fruit, some thirtyfold, some sixty, and some a hundred." We can see that affliction is one of the devil's tools which he uses against people.

"But, why?"

Specifically, he uses that tool on you to get the Word of God out of our heart. If Satan can keep our heart from getting full of the Word we will be ineffective in our Christian life.

Psalms 34:19 says "Many are the afflictions of the righteous, but the Lord delivers him out of them all." Our right standing with God, (that's what the word "righteous" means) is a threat to Satan's forces and plans. Because of our right standing with God, Satan cannot stop us, but we can stop him!! Oh, precious Christian, if we only knew, if we only believed how powerful we really are!!!!!!!

Satan does not want to be stopped or even slightly hindered. That's why he constantly attacks and undermines us. Because he is a liar, and a good one, he knows that the smartest thing he can do to neutralize us is to lie to us about what is happening to us, and divert our attention from what is really happening. If he can keep us busy thinking God is afflicting us or allowing us to be afflicted to teach us, or humble us, or perfect us, or force us to grow, we will never do anything for God, and we will never get out from under the constant attack of an ongoing string of afflictions.

eight
Does God Test Us?

Most of us have been taught our whole lives that God, from time to time, puts us through a variety of tests or trials to make us grow, to teach us something, to humble us. Christian leaders have been teaching that for so long, thinking it is logical, that I'm quite sure they completely believe it. In order to come to a Biblical understanding of this question, we will need to define some words, and look up some words in the Bible, to see what God says about them.

The English word "test" is not found in the King James Version of the Bible. You will find that word in other, more recent translations. This is due to the fact that the English language has changed since 1611, when James, King of England, authorized 70 scholars to make a translation of the Scriptures from the original languages, into the English spoken by the common people. The more recent translations use the more modern words. There is nothing about any of the translations that makes them more "Godly" or significant than the others.

In the King James Version, the words "tempt, "temptation," "tempted," and "tempter," mean "to test thoroughly," "to scrutinize," "to experiment with." Back in 1611, "tempt," meant to "test," but it doesn't mean the same thing at the beginning of the 21st century. Today, when we hear the word "tempted" we think of being lured or enticed to do something sinful. Here's the shocker—there is no such word in the entire Greek New Testament.

In the New Testament, the closest approximation we have of the concept of being "enticed" to do something sinful is found in James 1:14. "But every man is tempted, when he is drawn away of his own lust, and enticed." If any of us is being enticed to do something sinful, it is surely not God doing it. In fact it may not even be the devil! It is our own lust and depravity, convincing us that nobody will ever find out and that it will be OK, no matter what it is. The Bible says right there that in such a situation we will be "tempted". When our own lust draws us away and entices us to do the wrong thing, we will surely enter into a test of some kind. Rest assured that God did not engineer that set of events so He could see what kind of stuff is in us. He already knows that. We may also rest assured that God did not "allow" it for some mysterious purpose of His, which we could not possibly understand. He did not allow it—we brought it upon ourselves by giving in to our own selfishness and lust. When we are responsible for bringing on our own tests and trials, the test and trial is not the hard times and the junk we go through because of giving in to the lust and willfulness of our own heart. The true test that is happening there is to see whether or not we will believe the Word of God, and act upon it, rather than believing and acting upon the information in our own head.

The same is true when we are tempted by the devil. When the devil "tempts" someone, the "test" is the devil's effort to see if that person will fall for, and believe his lie, rather than believe the Word of God, and that ends up being sin.

Think about being "put to the test", or being "experimented with". Do we really think our Heavenly Father would do such a thing to us? Do we think He needs to do such a thing?

"But Pastor! Sometimes God just wants to find out what we're made of, doesn't He?"

Does God know everything? (The correct answer here is "Yes".) If He does, what is there about us that He doesn't know? (Correct answer is "Nothing".) If there is nothing He doesn't know about you, why does He need to find out anything? (Correct answer is, "He doesn't.")

"But Pastor, maybe He wants to show us what we're made of."

Does He need to "experiment" with us to show us that? Is there another way? (Correct answer is "Yes") What is there about us, and what we're made of, that the Word of God can't tell us? (Correct answer is "Nothing") Our Heavenly Father could not possibly gain either pleasure or glory by poking around on us like some kind of laboratory rat! We are His children, not His lab rats! If we, as earthly parents, did to our children what God, the Divine Parent, is accused of doing to His children, we would be locked up in a ward for the criminally insane. Is that the kind of Heavenly Father we think we have?

So, where do tests and trials come from? First let's look again at James 1:13. "Let no man say when he is tempted, I am tempted of God, for God cannot be tempted with evil, neither tempteth He any man." The first thing we know about our tests and trials, before we even need to look anywhere else, is that God is not doing it! "No man" includes you and me. No matter how it looks, or if we cannot figure any other way through it, back up and remember, "when I am going through a test or a trial, I should not say 'God is testing me', because we can't test God by using something evil, and God doesn't test anybody".

The second, and actually most logical, place to look is at the devil. Matthew 4:1 says. "Then was Jesus led up of the spirit into the wilderness to be tempted (tested) of the devil." In that same chapter, verse 3 says, "... and when the tempter (one who puts to the test) came to him ..." Mark 1:13 says, "And he was there in the wilderness forty days, tempted (tested) of Satan ..." Luke 4:2 says, "Being forty days tempted (tested) of the devil ..." 1 Thessalonians 3:5 says, "... lest by some means the tempter (one who puts to the test) have tempted (tested) you ..."

As we can see, the "If-God-Says-It-Once" Principle applied here will bring us quickly to a logical conclusion about our tests and trials. God is not doing it. God is not "allowing" it. The final chapter of this book details and describes what exactly it is that God "allows". You may be surprised.

The third place to look is at you. As we discussed before, James1: 14 says, "But every man is tempted (tested) when he is drawn away of his own lust and enticed." We need to make sure we understand that "lust" is not just talking about sex. Lust can be defined as "a natural desire that has gone beyond the proper boundaries." Any time we turn our natural desires loose to run freely until they reach their logical conclusion, we will be neck deep in more tests and trials than we can imagine!

The last part of 1 Corinthians 7:5 says, "... that Satan tempt (test) you not for your incontinency." The word "incontinency" means "no self control". This verse is in direct reference to sex between husband and wife, but the principle can be applied across the spectrum of human behaviors—if we do not exercise self-control, the devil will test us. The devil will also test us if we do exercise self control; it just won't be as hard on us—we'll see it coming and handle it rightly.

If we are in the midst of a test or a trial of some kind, the fourth and final place to look is at other people. Religious people are, far and away, the worst at "testing" each other. They will engineer an elaborate set of questions, or circumstances to either entrap each other, or prove their own rightness and superiority. At least the devil has a good reason for what he does. He wants to take over the throne of God and we are in the way—a speed bump on his road to success. He needs to make us dead so we will shut up, or he needs to make us ineffective so we will shut up. Either way works for him.

Religious people however are not so easy to figure out. One might think that since they are human we share a common enemy. Not so. For a person committed to Religion, anyone not adhering to that particular brand of religion is the enemy. Oddly enough, the devil agrees with them, especially where it concerns people whose main concern is a relationship with God rather than a particular religious practice.

Matthew 16:1 says "The Pharisees also with the Saducees, came and tempting, desired him that he would show them a sign from heaven." These political/religious people, enemies to each other, got together long enough to try to devise a plan to entrap Jesus. Matthew 19:3 shows us "The Pharisees also came unto him, tempting (testing) him, and saying unto him, 'is it lawful for a man to put away his wife for every cause?'" Again, religious people tried to get Jesus to choose sides in an ongoing religious argument, so they could use religious and political force as a means of controlling Him. Again, in Matthew 22:35, it says, "Then one of them, which was a lawyer, asked him a question, tempting (testing) him ..." Legalism is the strongest force religious people can exert, and in an effort to exert it, they will use words and "doctrinal issues" to trap us into being defensive. If we are unfortunate enough to get sucked into a religious debate with a legalistic person, and if he can get us on the defensive, he will soon render us speechless. Legalism is a destroyer, and from it, we should never expect mercy.

John 8:6 shows us some scribes and Pharisees who caught a woman in the very act of adultery. (If these guys were as spiritual as they told everyone they were, how did they know exactly who this woman was, exactly where she was and exactly what she was doing?) They came to Jesus spouting the Law, and asking Him what He thought about the Word of God. "This they said. Tempting (testing) him, that they might have to accuse him." Jesus was put to the test, to see if He would agree with the Word of God. The scribes and Pharisees tried to set Him up so they could accuse Him. He not only agreed with the Law, He when beyond it and let the Law accuse His accusers! He told them it would be OK to kill the girl, as long as the one among them who was without sin threw the first rock.

Jesus was tested often, and repeatedly, by Satan and by others, yet He consistently reacted without sin. When tests and trials come our way, and they surely will, what can we do about it? Paying attention closely to the next few pages could very well change our life.

First, let's look at Jesus, and how He handled the testing time Satan brought upon Him. Read Matthew 4:1-11 and specifically check out verse one. Jesus was "led up of the spirit into the wilderness to be tempted (tested) of the devil." The Holy Spirit is not the one who put Jesus through the testing time. He was the one who led Him out into the wilderness, knowing it was going to happen sooner or later. The Holy Spirit knew Satan was not patient enough to wait very long, so He got Jesus away from people, so when it did happen there would be no innocent casualties standing by.

See verse 2! Jesus fasted for 40 days, and after that time period he was "hungry", and without a doubt, weak.

Read verse 3! When Jesus was at his weakest point, the "one

who puts to the test showed up, trying to trap Him ("if thou be ...") and make Him doubt the provision of God ("... command that these stones be made bread.")

Look at verse 4! "But He answered and said, 'It is written, Man shall not live by bread alone, but by every word that proceedeth out of the mouth of God.'" Jesus used a simple, scriptural, one-liner to smash that test. Notice He didn't have to quote several chapters to get the devil to knock it off, nor did He have to give "chapter and verse" for what He said! Satan knows when it's the Word, and he knows when you don't know what you're talking about. Running off at the mouth, copping an attitude, and getting angry does not get rid of the devil. One sentence, Solid Word, spoken in faith = End Of Test, Passing Grade!

Check out verse 5! "Then the devil taketh him up into the holy city, and setteth him on a pinnacle of the temple, ..." Satan gave Jesus a supernatural transportation experience (impressive, no?).

What about verse 6? "And saith unto him, 'If thou be the Son of God, cast thyself down: for it is written, 'He shall give his angels charge concerning thee: and in their hands they shall bear thee up, lest at any time thou dash thy foot against a stone.'" Satan tried to TRAP Jesus ("if thou be ...") into doing something foolish—"Jump, the Bible says the angels will catch you, (heh, heh.)". Did you notice that he even quoted scripture to make the whole thing sound more spiritual, and therefore more convincing?

Go on to verse 7! "Jesus said unto him, 'It is written again, 'Thou shalt not tempt the Lord thy God.'" Jesus hammered another test with just eight words!! One sentence, Solid Word, spoken in faith = End Of Test, Passing Grade!

Then there's verse 8! "Again, the devil taketh him up into an exceeding high mountain, and sheweth him all the kingdoms of the world, and the glory of them;" Another supernatural transportation experience, even more impressive than the last one.

Watch out, here comes verse 9! "And saith unto him, 'All these things will I give thee, if thou wilt fall down and worship me.'" Satan tried to trap ("if thou wilt ..." and "... I will give ...") Jesus into worshipping him!

Here comes verse 10! "Then saith Jesus unto him, 'Get thee

hence, Satan: for it is written, 'Thou shalt worship the Lord thy God, and him only shalt thou serve.'" Jesus said "Beat it, creep!" (A little poetic license, there) and gave him another Scriptural one-liner. One sentence, Solid Word, spoken in faith = End Of Test, Passing Grade!

Results time! See verse 11! "Then the devil leaveth him, and, behold, angels came and ministered unto him." It Works!!!!! Hallelujah, It Works!

The bottom line is this: Go to the Word of God, find an answer, and speak the answer, don't waste time whining about the problem. Everybody knows there's a problem. We've all got problems. Welcome to the planet. Do something constructive about it.

There are several salient facts that we need to know well if we expect not to fall for the devil's lying tests.

1 Corinthians 10:13 is a familiar, but much misunderstood passage of scripture. First let me explain the misunderstanding. "There is no temptation (test) taken you, but such as is common to man: but God is faithful, who will not suffer you to be tempted (tested) above that ye are able, but will, with the temptation (test) also make a way to escape, that ye may be able to bear it." The common statement we have all heard is that "God will not give you more problems than you can handle." That thought comes from the phrase in the verse, "... will not suffer you to be tempted, above that ye are able, but will, with the temptation also make a way to escape ..."

The misunderstanding in this verse has its foundation in the thought that God is the one who gives the problem/pressure/trouble/ heartache/ test/tragedy/trial in the first place. Taking that error out of our understanding of that verse, let's look at what it actually says. "There is no temptation (test) that has overtaken you but such as is common to man". Do you see that? Satan can not—God won't let him—use his vast backlog of experience to create some new test for us. He can only use the things that are common to human beings.

"God is faithful (the Greek word means "trustworthy"), who will not suffer (the Greek word means "allow") you to be tempted (put to the test) above that ye are able ..." God will not allow the devil to bring a test or trial upon you that is absolutely too much for you.

What is it that you cannot do? Philippians 4:13 says, "I can do all things through Christ who strengtheneth me." There is no doubt that we can do (The Greek word translated "do" means "be, make, cause to happen, endure, bear up under") anything because of Jesus inside us. His belief in our ability far exceeds our own. "... but will, with the temptation (test) provide a way to escape ..."

When the test comes upon us, it is not because God wills it, or allows it, but He knows it is coming, so when it appears, He has provided, within the test, a means of making it go away, or helping us get through it successfully. He does this so that we will be able to bear it. (The Greek word means to "bear up under it, endure it, do it, cause something to happen about it.")

The Bottom Line: When a test or trial comes, know this—it is not anything bigger than you can handle.

The second thing we need to know when a test comes, is shown to us in James 1:2. "My brethren, count it all joy when you fall into divers (various) temptations (tests)." We must know that when a test or a trial comes into our life we can make a withdrawal from our joy account. According to Galatians 5:22, joy is a manifestation of the fruit of the Spirit. The Holy Spirit is in us. His joy is in us along with Him. Nehemiah 8:10 says, "... the joy of the Lord is your strength." His joy is not connected to our feelings, nor is it connected to our circumstances! Happiness is a feeling, and is directly related to our circumstances. Joy is a force of the Spirit, and if we let it, it will have an impact on our circumstances.

The very next verse, James 1:3 says, "knowing this, that the trying of your faith worketh patience." We will be able to count it all joy if we know this. This, then, is the third thing we need to know, deep in our knower: The test is not a test of us personally, it is a test of our faith. Remember, "Faith cometh by hearing, and hearing by the Word of God." (Romans 10:17). When a test of our faith comes, it is really a test of how much and how well we are hearing the Word of God in order to make our faith a strong force in your life.

I find it interesting that, although Satan knows it is not personal, he does everything he can to make it feel personal. So, precious heart, even though the test feels personal, it is not. And, if that were not good enough news, that very test can, if we so desire, put Patience to work. Notice it does not say it produces patience. (Yes, I do know that some translations say that, but the Greek words that make up this phrase, literally translated, mean, "patience put to work") The word "patience" is a Greek word meaning "consistency". There is only one thing that is absolutely the same all the time. Since it isn't me, nor is it you, nor is it anyone's favorite denomination, or guru, it must be something else. The Word of God!

No matter what else changes, the Word will say the same thing all the time! If I'm sick, the Word says, "By His stripes ye were healed." If I'm well, the Word says, "By His stripes ye were healed." If I die, the Word will still say, "By His stripes ye were healed." If we can keep our mouth disciplined to speak the Word, we will not only continuously build our faith, we will allow our patience to go to work for us. In truth, whether or not we exercise any patience is a matter of our will, not God's will.

James 1:4 tells us to "... let patience have her perfect work ..." If we don't let the patience that already exists on the inside of us do its work, it won't!

"But Pastor! I'm not very patient! I prayed and prayed for God to give me more patience, and all I got was more problems!"

Patience is not connected to your problems in any way but a merely peripheral sense. Patience is connected to your spirit. Your flesh has the problems!

The fruit of the Spirit is manifested as "patience" or "long-suffering", (neither of which means "suffer a long time, then die disappointed"), according to Galatians 6:22. Just like the spaghetti sauce — "It's in there"! Praying for God to give us patience, makes about as much sense as asking God to give us a brain—we've already got it!! Whether or not we use it, is up to us. It is exactly like that with patience.

The last half of James 1:4 tells us that once we let patience have her "perfect" (the Greek word means "complete, mature, or maturing") "work" in us, it will make us "perfect" (same word), "and entire" (the Greek word means "perfectly sound or whole"), "wanting" (the Greek word means "lacking") nothing!!!

nine
What Does God Use to Chasten, Reprove, Teach and Perfect us?

It is obvious that God does indeed chasten us, reprove us, teach us, and desire to perfect us. What is not so obvious and what is indeed a source of some confusion in the Body of Christ, is how He does it. In this chapter we will look at all four of these areas: chastening, reproving, teaching, and perfecting. Each of these areas will be seen in the light of how God gets each of them accomplished in the lives of His people.

The first thing to look at, which underlies a good understanding of this whole discussion, is the fact that God is the father of our spirit. Hebrews 12:9 clearly distinguishes between the father of our flesh and the father of our spirit. "Furthermore, we have had fathers of our flesh which corrected us, and we gave them reverence: shall we not much rather be in subjection to the father of spirits, and live?" God is not the father of my flesh. I have the same pointed nose and receding hairline as my Dad, Rusty Anderson.

Way back, a long time ago God created human beings and made it so that when a sperm cell and an egg got together in the womb, another human being would form with the combined physical attributes of both parents. God is the father of my spirit. Rusty is the father of my flesh.

My father, Rusty, like all fathers everywhere, found the need to correct me for one kind of infraction or another, from time to time.

Even though some of my problems were rooted in spiritual matters, there was nothing in the natural he could do to reach my spirit. Now, I know that the human spirit can be hurt and locked up because of things that are done to us in the flesh. I also know that this same human spirit is incredibly tougher than we give it credit for being, most of the time. All my dad could do was take my body to task for what I had done; hoping the consequences would hurt bad enough to create a change in undesired behavior. I have been spanked, slapped, back-handed, kicked, beaten with belts and coat-hangers, and several other ingenious articles, but the only effect those things had on my spirit was to make it defensive and closed up.

Conversely, God is not the father of my body, so He cannot deal with my spirit through it—He can only deal with my spirit. God only deals with people on a spiritual level. If our car begins to get poor gas mileage, would we take a big hammer and pound great dents into the hood and doors, and smash out all the glass, just to teach it a lesson? Of course not! We are smarter than to think that such a thing would work. We would work on the things on the inside of the engine, which we know would improve the poor performance, wouldn't we? Isn't it reasonable to assume that the God of the Universe is at least as smart as we are????

You are a spirit, you have a soul, and you live in a body. We are not our body, even though that is the part of us everyone sees and recognizes. Our body is just our "earth suit." When people leave this atmosphere and go into space, they must travel in a "space ship" and work out in hard vacuum in a "space suit." That space suit gives them a right to be out there, and the ability to survive there. Our "earth suit" gives us the right to be on this earth, and the ability to survive here. When the "life support" leaks out of our earth suit and the suit dies, we must leave—we no longer have a right to be here, or the ability to survive here. Our natural habitat is heaven, if we have made Jesus Christ our Lord, and hell, if we have not

We are not our soul, either. Our soul is the compilation of our mind, our will, our intellect and our emotions. Those things are our possessions, not our identity. They are the primary means through which we give and receive communication while occupying our earth suit.

Does God chasten His children? Yes!! Hebrews 12:6 tells us that "whom the Lord loveth, he chasteneth, and scourgeth every son whom he receiveth." When God, the Father of our spirit "chastens" us, it is because He loves us too much to leave us the way we are. Thankfully, He loves us just the way we are, but He doesn't want to leave us the way we are.

There are eight different Hebrew words that have been translated into English as "chasten." They mean "convince," "reason together," "rebuke," "correct," "instruct," "reprove," "teach,"

There are six Greek words translated "chasten." They mean, "to convince," "to educate," "tutor," "instruction," "teach," "train."

Go back and notice each of those words, both Greek and Hebrew, from the New Testament, and the Old Testament. None of them is a "physical" word. Not one of those words denotes any kind of physical enactment at all.

"But Pastor! What about the word 'scourge'?"

That word means "to whip" and the root word for that Greek word means "to squeeze". Christian people run afoul of that word when they misunderstand what part of the real you God works on. If we believe that God beats up on our body to make some improvements to our spirit (remember the car?), we will apply that word, "scourgeth", to any variety of physical mis-happenstance. If we understand that God is the father of our spirit, and therefore will "scourge" us on that level, we will understand that for God to "whip" us and "squeeze" us in the spirit may very well be the most uncomfortable thing we have ever endured.

Hebrews 12:10 tells that the fathers of our flesh "... verily for a few days chastened us after their own pleasure ..." but God chastens us "... for our profit, that we might be partakers of his holiness." Can we hear that?? God chastens us so that we can better partake of His holiness! Think about it! It can't be physical! Have you ever been in a fight, and lost? You got beat up? Tell me, did it make you more holy? Absolutely not! It didn't even make you a better fighter! If we cannot make each other more holy by beating on each others' bodies, God cannot make us more holy using the same means. Do you know anyone who is more holy because of cancer, arthritis, car wrecks, or heart attacks? I know people that are more hurt and more dead because of those things, but none that are more holy.

"But Pastor! My dear old Aunt Crusty has arthritis, and heart trouble, and she is really holy. She yells at everybody about God, all the time."

Is she HOLY, or just religiously grouchy? If she actually is walking in more holiness than she was before, it is only because she is spending more time in the Word, not because she is sick. Sickness does not make us holy, it makes us dead.

Hebrews 12:9 gives us the key to "the chastening of the Lord" and what makes it work in our lives. We are instructed to "… be in subjection to the father of spirits, and live?" We must submit ourselves to the Father, and His discipline of our spirit. If we do, we will "live".

Does God teach His children? Yes!!

There are five Hebrew words translated "reprove," or "reproof." They mean, "chide," "correct," "argue," "refute," "reason together." The last one is the same word that is translated in other places as "chasten." Notice again that there are no "physical" words here.

There are two Greek words translated "reprove" or "reproof." They mean "to admonish" and "to tell a fault". Notice again, the complete absence of any "physical" words.

Proverbs 1:23 is the wisdom (Word) of God speaking to us: "Turn you at my reproof: behold, I will pour out my spirit unto you, I will make known my words unto you." God does reprove us, but He does it by His Word, and His Holy Spirit, and we must turn to it on our own. God will not make us turn to His Word. If He were to make anybody do something, He would make everyone get saved!

"But Pastor! What if we don't turn to His reproof? Doesn't He need to resort to stronger measures to get us to do what He wants?"

Please keep in mind that God is not a larger, more powerful version of human. He is much more mature than we are, and He has no need whatever to insist on His own right-ness in order for things to be OK with Him.

Proverbs 1:30-33 — "They would none of my counsel: they despised all my reproof. Therefore shall they eat of the fruit of their own way, and be filled with their own devices. For the turning away of the simple (foolish, seducible) shall slay them, and the prosperity of fools shall destroy them. But whoso hearkeneth unto me shall dwell safely, and shall be quiet from fear of evil." If we don't turn to God's reproof, we will eat the fruit of our own way— destruction, and death. If we do turn to His reproof, we can expect to "dwell safely," and be "quiet from fear of evil." Destruction of any kind is not God's reproof; it is the result of not turning to God's reproof—His Word!

Does God teach His people? Yes!! Nobody in the Body of Christ doubts that, but there is some confusion about how He does it. Does He use the "two-by-four-to-the-forehead method?" Does He use the "rat-in-the-maze method?" Is it possible that there may be yet another way God has of getting His point across?

We can see clearly in John 14:26, Who does the teaching, and How: "But the comforter, which is the Holy Ghost, whom the Father will send in my name, he shall teach you all things, and bring all things to your remembrance, whatsoever I have said unto you." The Holy Spirit shows us whatsoever Jesus has said (the Word of God). If we are not reading and/or hearing the Word of God, there is painfully little He can do for us. If we want to hear the Word and feed our faith, God has given us a series of "gifts."

Ephesians 4:11 — "And he gave some apostles (a ministry of the Word), and some prophets (a ministry of the Word), and some, evangelists (a ministry of the Word), and some, pastors (a ministry of the Word), and teachers (a ministry of the Word)." God set ministries of the Word into the Body of Christ to teach us the Word. There is no where in the entire Bible, that states that God uses any other means to teach anyone, other than His Word.

Does God want to perfect His people? Yes!! In Genesis 17:1, God said, "... walk before me and be thou perfect." In Matthew 5: 48 said, "Be ye therefore perfect, even as your Father, which is in heaven is perfect."

"Perfect???"

If God thought that word meant "flawless", He is destined for a life of total disappointment. He does demand perfection, but the Greek word that is translated "perfect" means, "to be entire," "whole," "completely sound and mature." God expects us to strive to be whole, entire, sound, mature people. Since this is clearly what God expects of us, there must be a way to make it happen.

We just read in Ephesians 4:11, how that God gave us ministries of the Word, such as apostles, prophets, evangelists, pastors and teachers. As we read on in the two verses that follow, we'll see why He gave those gifts: "for the perfecting (maturing) of the saints for the work of the ministry, for the edifying (building up) of the Body of Christ, until we all come in the unity of the faith, and of the knowledge of the Son of God, unto a perfect man, unto the measure of stature of the fullness of Christ:"

He gave some apostles, prophets, evangelists and pastors and teachers—ministries of the Word—for the perfecting (maturing, completing, making whole) of the saints! Notice He did not give problems, tests, trials, hardships and tragedies to perfect us, He gave ministries of the Word. The purpose of these ministries is to unite us in our faith, which comes by hearing, and hearing by the Word of God (Romans 10:17), and to fill us with the knowledge of the Son of God. Knowledge of the Son of God comes only from the Word of God. As we turn to the Word, and let the Word discipline us and correct us, and make us mature, we will become "a perfect man, unto the measure of the stature of the fullness of Christ."

We can see it clearly. It is the Word that chastens us. It is the Word that reproves us. It is the Word that teaches us. It is the Word that brings us into a place of maturity. Since it is the Word that does it all, let's look at 2 Timothy 3:16-17 to see God's answer to this whole question.

"All scripture is given by inspiration of God, and is profitable for doctrine, for reproof, for correction, for instruction in righteousness: that the man of God may be perfect, thoroughly furnished unto all good works."

The term translated "inspiration of God" comes from two Greek words, "theo," meaning "God," and "pneustos," meaning "breathed." Hold your hand in front of your face, and speak. You can feel your breath as it hits your hand. We must breathe in order to speak. We will get more out of our Bible if we treat it as though, every time we open it's pages, God is speaking so directly with us, that we can feel His breath on our face as He speaks.

The Word is profitable — (the Greek word means "valuable, worth something, or advantageous)! When we are trying to read the Word, and the devil is telling us it's boring and a waste of time, and our flesh is agreeing with the devil, we must remind the devil, and our flesh that the Word is profitable! What is it profitable for?

The Word is profitable for doctrine. Doctrine does not mean "believe-it-my-way-or-else". All it means is "clear, straight, and organized thinking". Doctrine is not bad stuff that was created to confuse young Christians. It is simply a way to clear up our thinking. If one doctrine or another becomes such an important issue that it starts to become either a weapon or a wall of division, it is time to repent.

It is profitable for reproof, which does not mean that any of us has the right to use the Word as our personal club for getting the world or the church into our definition of shape. The Word is not for us to use to attack one another; it is for us to turn to, for our own reproof. Simply put, if we need to be chewed out, the Word is God's way of doing it.

It is profitable for correction. Too often believers take it upon themselves to play Holy-Ghost-And-Interpreter-Of-The-Word, and try to fix their fellow believers. Through the Word, God will show us what we are doing wrong, and how to fix it in ourselves. Another nice thing about the Word is that, when God shows us something we are doing wrong, He will do it in love.

It is profitable for instruction in righteousness, which does not mean, "how-to-be-as-right-as-I-am". The Word is the only place where God shows us what we have, and who we are, as a result of being in Jesus.

Christian, God has given us His Word, and it is profitable, to make us mature, and thoroughly furnished unto all good works. God has given us everything it takes to grow us up, and totally equip us to do anything. If there is something missing in your Christian experience, it is not because God left it out.

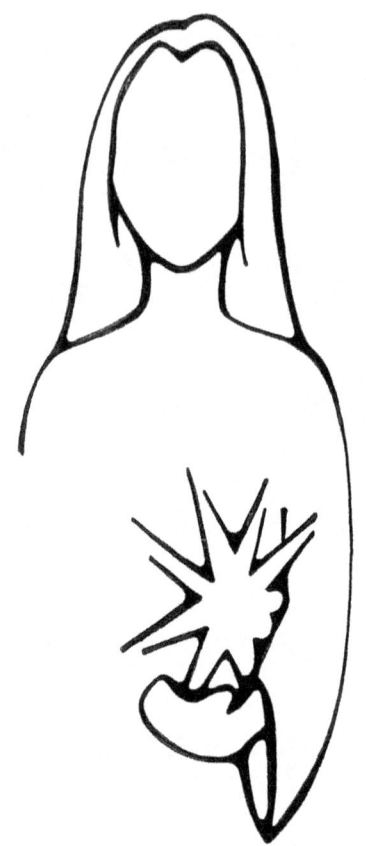

ten
What Has God Done For us In Jesus?

I have mentioned several times up to this point that we need to know what God has done for us because of Jesus, and yet I haven't discussed what some of those things are. Let's do that now, keeping in mind that this is not designed to be a total and all-encompassing study on the matter. This chapter is only designed to whet our appetite and send us digging deeper for more.

1 Corinthians 1:30 puts it in a nice, neat nutshell for us: "But of him are ye in Christ Jesus, who of God is made unto us wisdom, and righteousness, and sanctification and redemption."

What that verse says, in language a little easier to follow, is this: Because of God, we are in Christ Jesus, and God has made Jesus-in-us wisdom to us, therefore we are wise. God has made Jesus-in-us righteousness to us, therefore we are righteous. God has made Jesus-in-us sanctification to us, therefore we are holy. God has made Jesus-in-us redemption to us, therefore we are free.

This verse says that Jesus is "made unto us" righteousness. 2 Corinthians 5:21 says, "that we might be made the righteousness of God in him." We must know that when God makes something, He doesn't do a half-baked job of it. Romans 3:22 tells us that the righteousness of God has come "... unto all, and upon all them that believe ..." God's righteousness, given to us when we received Jesus, has come upon all who believe—not some, not a few—all.

The next thing God has done for us in Jesus is that He has given us authority now, not later. In Matthew 28:18-19, we see Jesus telling the disciples that "All power is given to me, in heaven and in earth, Go ye therefore ..." The Greek word "exhousia," translated "power" in this passage of Scripture literally means "authority."

I took a piece of paper, wrote down the quote shown above, and showed it to an attorney friend of mine, asking him to tell me what legal principle those words described. He glanced at the words and said, "Power of Attorney. This is a very good description of a working, specific Power of Attorney document."

To put this into a rather more homey example, let's say that Farmer Jones says to his friend, Ronny, "All of $10,000 has been given unto me by the banker. Go ye therefore, to the sale barn and buy pigs." That is a specific use for a specific dollar amount, and the legal right to carry it out. Ronny knows that he cannot spend more than $10,000, and that he should not spend less. Ronny also knows that if he tries to come back with a load of walnuts or chickens, the deal is off. He used the money, but not for the right purpose.

Jesus has been given all authority in heaven, and all authority in earth, and He delegated it all to you, for a specific purpose. You (I, us, we, y'all, us'n's, all y'all, and all o' us'n) are supposed to take the all and go to all nations—known in the popular vernacular as "everywhere"—and baptize people, and teach them everything the Word of God says. When we do that, Jesus has promised to go with us. If we decide to go nowhere and do nothing He probably won't be much help to us in getting that particular project done. If we go and do, we'll never have to go and do alone. If we don't go and do, we'll have to deal with all of it ourselves.

Ephesians 2:6 tells us that we now "... sit together with him in heavenly places in Christ Jesus." Does anybody who is sitting in heavenly places put up with a lot of garbage? Do they think diseases are normal? Do they think that the things which may come against them have a right to succeed? We, as the earthly membership of the Body of Christ, need to learn to believe we actually possess the authority Jesus said He gave to us. If we don't believe that, we'll get our tender little self kicked all over the neighborhood, and we'll think it's normal.

Too many Christians are ignorant of who they are, and what that means. God wants us to know!!!

Ephesians 1:18-23 says we are supposed to "know" the "hope of his calling," as well as "the riches of the glory of his inheritance" in us. We are supposed to "know" the "exceeding greatness of his power" (the Greek word is "dunamis" which means "explosive, or miraculous power") "to usward who believe, according to the working of his mighty power" (the Greek word "exhousia" means "authority").

Colossians 2:12 shows us that we were "Buried with him in baptism, wherein also ye are risen with him through the faith of the operation of God, who hath raised him from the dead." The power of God in us is the same power that He used when He raised Jesus from the dead, and it works by His faith! God, by faith, believes that we were raised from the dead with Jesus!

Back to Ephesians 1: Verse 21 shows us that God set Jesus down (and us in Him) "Far above all principality and power, and might and dominion, and every name that is named, not only in this world, but also in that which is to come." Because we are in Christ, we are in a position that is "far above" any power, of either man or devil—Act Like It!! Verses 22 and 23 show us that "all things" have been put "under His feet," and that He is the "head over all things to the church, which is his body." He is the head, the church is His body, and all things are under His feet. The last time I checked my feet were still a part of my body. That puts "all things" under us, by the operation of the faith of God. That means God believes a LOT better things concerning us than we do!!

Matthew 10:1—Jesus gave His disciples "... power "exhousia" against unclean spirits, to cast them out, and to heal all manner of sickness, and all manner of disease."

Read Mark 16:15-18. We can see that Jesus gave a specific group of people—"them that believe"—authority to carry out a rather wide spectrum of activities. The list includes, "... preaching the gospel to every creature, casting out devils, speaking with new tongues, ... " dealing with, and being protected from naturally harmful animals, being protected from enemies trying to poison them, "... laying hands on the sick ... " and expecting them to "... recover ... " All that stuff is included in the authority delegated to believers.

Another thing God has done for us in Jesus is He has redeemed us now, not later. Both Ephesians 1:7, and Colossians 1:14 say, "In whom we have redemption ... " In whom (Jesus) we have (present tense) redemption. Hebrews 9:12 says Jesus "... obtained (past tense) eternal redemption for us." Galatians 3: 13-14 says "Christ hath (past tense) redeemed us from the curse of the law ... so that the blessing of Abraham might come on the gentiles through Jesus Christ." If you want to know what the "curse of the law" is, in a nutshell, read Deuteronomy 28:15-68. If you want to know what the "blessing of Abraham" is, read Deuteronomy 28:1-14.

The letters of Paul to the early churches are filled with phrases like "in him," "in whom," "by whom," "by Christ Jesus," "in Christ Jesus," etc. etc. In fact, there are no fewer than 133 of this kind of phrases! Again, I think the "If-God-says-something-once" principle applies here. These verses were designed by God to give us a revelation of who we are because of Jesus, and what we can do because of what Jesus has done.

The letters of Paul contain the word "righteousness" exactly 269% more often than the rest of the New Testament. All these things are ours by birthright. We should do ourselves a favor, and build them into our heart very carefully and purposefully. How do we build something into ourselves until it becomes an instinctive part of our walk? Meditate it. Mutter it. Chew it. Speak it out loud, over and over and over and over and over and over and over and over and over and over and over ... Get the hint?

eleven
What Can We Do Because Of What Jesus Has Done?

Once we know what God has done for us in Jesus, the next, most logical question is "What does that mean I can do?"

Philippians 4:13 says, "I can do all things through Christ which strengtheneth me." What does "all things" not include? Nothing!! If we are looking for a good blanket statement, this is it!! We can do anything!!!!!

"But Pastor, does that mean I can do all kinds of illegal stuff and Jesus will help me?"

Of course Jesus is not going to help us break the law, or hurt people (ourselves included)!! He will however, help us do the more important and much more exciting stuff. Stuff like preaching the Good News. He will help us do stuff like pray and get Results with a Capital R. He will show us how to cast out devils, raise the dead, heal the sick, speak with new tongues, pray the perfect will of God, and lots of other, really cool stuff.

In Luke 10:17, we see the disciples getting really excited about making things happen by using the name of Jesus. They came back to the JC and the Boys Evangelistic Association ministry headquarters and reported that "... even the devils are subject to us through thy name." We don't have to take a bunch of stuff from the devil; we can put a stop to him. Remember Paul? God will not do for us what we have the power and ability to do for ourselves. That is a lot.

Jesus told us in John 14:13-14, "And whatsoever ye shall ask in my name, that will I do, that the father may be glorified in the son. If ye shall ask anything in my name, I will do it." These two verses tell us that if we pray in Jesus name we can expect results. The word translated "ask," is the Greek word that means "demand". Now, before the brain goes into "Religious Tilt", and we begin to imagine that I'm advocating that we start "bossing God around" in some fashion or another, please know that I am not doing any such thing. In the Scriptures, I find only one individual crazy enough to do that. He got kicked out of Heaven for thinking about it—before he even got a chance to try it!

I am neither suggesting that we demand anything from God, nor that we treat Him like a slave sent to do our bidding, nor that we behave like ill-mannered children towards Him. However, once we know what the will of God is, we can stand firm and demand that we, the devil and our circumstances conform to the will of God. That is what we demand, and from whom we demand it.

John 15:16 tells us that part of the command to "... go and bring forth fruit ..." is "that whatsoever ye shall ask of the Father in my name, he may give it you." The Greek word translated "ask" in this verse means "to request". At the end of the verse, where it says, "he may give it you," does not mean that "he may, or may not give it to us, depending on whatever He decides". What it does mean is that He has chosen and ordained us so that we would produce fruit. In doing so, He wants us to make request in the name of Jesus. The word "may" means "to have permission to act," in other words, when we make request of the Father in the Name of Jesus, He has our permission to act on our behalf. If we will do that, He is, by our faith in and use of the name of Jesus, able to answer our prayers, and grant our requests.

Because of what Jesus has done, we have the right to use our faith on purpose, and expect it to produce. Let's look through Mark 11:22-24 and see how this works.

"And Jesus answering saith unto them, 'Have faith in God.'" Another translation says in that spot, "have the faith of God." It makes sense to me, that if we are supposed to have faith in God, we should use the same kind of faith He uses and apply it the same way He does. "For verily I say unto you, 'That whosoever shall say unto this mountain, 'Be thou removed, and be thou cast into the sea;'" If we have the same kind of faith God has, and use it the same way He does, we will speak words of faith directly to our obstacles. God, in faith, speaks directly to whatever He wants moved or changed, and He tells it exactly what He wants it to do. "And shall not doubt in his heart, but shall believe that those things which he saith shall come to pass, he shall have whatsoever he saith." We need not feel that our faith must encompass everything we are speaking. The spiritual law is, "he shall have whatsoever he saith". The truth of the matter is that whether your words are good ones, or bad ones, they will eventually bear fruit in your life. The fact is, whether you believe that or not, it will still be true. It is a law.

The nature of a law is that it works all the time. If we do believe that we will have what we say, it should change the way we speak. We don't have to totally believe everything we say, just have enough of a "mustard seed" of faith to believe that what we say will happen. That takes a lot of the pressure off!! "Therefore I say unto you, what things so ever ye desire, when ye pray, believe that ye receive them, and ye shall have them." If we have nerve enough to believe that whatever we have asked has been granted, we can and should give thanks for it, and we will eventually see it in our hot little hand.

Mark 16:15-18 gives us a clear picture of the way normal Christianity is supposed to look. "And He said unto them, Go ye into all the world, and preach the gospel to every creature." Normal Christians are gospel-sharing Christians. Statistics tell us that only about 5% of the Body of Christ have ever led one person to Christ. That makes about 95% of the Body of Christ, living and obeying the Scriptures at somewhere less than normal!! WOW! God thinks it is normal to present the Good News everywhere we go! "And these signs will follow them that believe ..." Mark 16:20 says, "And they went forth, and preached everywhere, the Lord working with them, and confirming the Word with signs following." Signs follow the Word, when we believe enough to step out and become "doers of the Word" (James 1:22).

"What can we expect to do?"

So glad you asked.

"In my name shall they cast out devils." God thinks it is normal for His children to deal with the devil with authority and confidence. It is decidedly not normal for His people to be afraid of the devil.

"They shall speak with new tongues ... " God thinks it's normal for His children to speak and pray with new tongues. Relax!! Nobody, including God is telling anybody they have to speak in tongues. It is simply a gift. Nothing more. Nothing less. If we decide we don't want or need that gift for whatever reason, That's OK. That doesn't make us some kind of second-class Christian. We have all the same equipment and opportunities that any other Christian has. Those of us who do speak in tongues, using that gift does not make us a BETTER Christian (or worse, for that matter). I know plenty of flaky people who speak in tongues. I also know plenty of flaky people who don't. Speaking in tongues or not speaking in tongues, is no kind of a badge of spiritual maturity. It is a gift—nothing more, nothing less. We don't have to speak in tongues; we can if we want to. Some of us are afraid of this little gift, because we think it may make us do something weird — don't worry about it. Some of us don't believe we need this gift — don't worry about it. "These signs follow them that believe ..." We've got to believe it, in order for it to happen to us at all!"

"They shall take up serpents." I don't find any support at all in the Scriptures for messing with a harmful creature, just to test a person's faith. However, as we are going about the business of normal Christianity, if we encounter a naturally harmful animal, we have a right to trust God to keep us safe! (See Paul in Acts 28:1-6 and Daniel in Daniel chapter 6.)

"And if they drink any deadly thing, it shall not hurt them ..." Again, I find no support in the Scriptures for drinking poison, just to test our faith. I also find no support in the Scriptures for drinking as much harmful stuff as we want because it tastes good, or picks us up, or whatever, and then expecting God to fix the adverse effects of our foolishness. If, in the course of going about the business of a normal Christian life, someone hates us badly enough to try to kill us by poison, we have a right to expect God to protect us.

"They shall lay their hands on the sick, and they shall recover." We have a right to expect that when we lay our hands on a sick person, they will recover! This is normal Christianity.

We see in Romans 8:31, "If God be for us, who can be against us." How can we possibly let the devil stop us? God is on our side! When the enemy comes against us, we can use the name of Jesus to control Satan's activity, and impact our contrary circumstances. Matthew 12:29 says, "... or else how can one enter into a strong man's house, and spoil his goods, except he first bind the strong man? And then he will spoil his house." If the devil has stolen something or someone from us, we can go take it back. You bind the strong man and you spoil his house—friends don't let friends go to hell.

Romans 8:37 says, "Nay, in all these things ..." What things? Go back a bit and read verses 35 and 36. Things like "tribulation," "distress," "persecution," "famine," "nakedness," "peril," "sword," "for thy sake we are killed all the day long; we are accounted as sheep for the slaughter." Verse 37 goes on to say "... we are more than conquerors through him that loved us." The Greek phrase that is translated "we are more than conquerors" literally means, "we over-conquer". Are you familiar with the concept of "over-kill?" This is what happens when a housewife takes the largest encyclopedia she can find and pushes it with all her might onto the unsuspecting frame of a spider who was found, ill-advisedly crawling across one of her walls. It does not take that much force to kill that spider, but she uses it all anyway. That's over-kill.

Because of what Jesus has done and all the power of God He has put at our disposal, we over-conquer in all these things. There is no such thing as a bad day that can whip us. There is no attack that can win against us. The only problem that can cause any of the things arrayed against us to succeed, is an attitude problem. We Christians spend more time beating ourselves up, and defeating ourselves, than we spend being beat up and defeated by the devil. Here's the big dilemma, and it is both big, and a dilemma, because we do not believe either half of it: The devil is already defeated, and we are undefeatable!

twelve
What Does God Allow?

All of my life, I have heard about the various things God "allows" for a variety of reasons. Things like diseases, accidents, fears, tragedies of all kinds, and death of every description are all "allowed" by God for reasons known only to Him. If we ever do figure out the answer, it will only be much later. Much too later to do any good or make the lesson worth while.

This is such strong teaching across the breadth of the Body of Christ, and so pervasive, that I just had to address it. Many Bible teachers don't ever go to the Bible and search out exactly what the Bible says, "God allows". Mostly, they have just thought about what happened, to themselves or someone else. They then decided that there must be some kind of reason for it, but they're not sure what it may be. The next logical step goes something like this: Since God knows everything, and God controls everything, he must have allowed it to happen for some reason. The problem with that thinking is that, even though it sounds spiritual, it has a couple of major flaws.

The first flaw is that the person giving that out as an answer to a tough situation did not go the Bible to find out exactly what "God Allows". Since I couldn't find anyone who had done that, I decided to look it up for myself—I was SHOCKED! If the way everyone talked about it was an indicator, there should have been hundreds of verses, giving lists of things God will allow for spiritual reasons, all over the place!

What I found was a grand total of one verse using the phrase "allowed of God". ONE. One. 1. That is as startling to me by its lack of support, as some other things are by their overwhelming support. That one verse must be a real doozy. It must be such a staggering revelation that the entire mind and heart of man can bear no more than one. It is found in 1 Thessalonians 2:4.

"But as we were allowed of God to be put in trust with the gospel, even so we speak; not as pleasing men, but God, which trieth our hearts." This is the only place in the entire Bible that says that God allows anything at all, and it says He allows us to be entrusted with the Word of God. WOW!! He didn't "allow" accidents, diseases and heartaches for some mysterious purpose. He "allows" us to handle His Word. That is a huge departure from what I had always been taught.

By the way, the word "trieth" in that verse is a Greek word that means "discerns" or "approves". That word does not mean, "puts to the test". God has allowed us to handle His Word because He approves of our heart.

The other major flaw in thinking is the thought that God "controls" everything. It is a rather comforting thought, to think He controls everything, because it gives Him all the responsibility, and me, none. Let's lay a brief foundation for fixing that flaw.

We discussed Matthew 28:18 before, in which Jesus delegates to us "All authority in heaven and in earth", and tells us to "Go ye, therefore". Jesus gave us authority—a lot of authority—and a specific command to go somewhere and do something with it. What is authority for? There is only one thing it is good for, and only one thing it works for—control. How much authority did Jesus give? "All authority in heaven and earth". If God were in control of everything and everyone, why would He need to give any control and authority to us?

If God really is supposed to be controlling everything, I think He should be fired, for lousy job performance! Come on! Let's open our eyes! Can't we see the mess we are living in?? Be honest. If God created that, or even if He allowed it to happen, it is so incredibly sloppy that the rest of the universe must be nearly ready to enter total collapse.

No.

God is not in control of everything and everyone. He has given control over to us, but unlike us, when He gives someone authority, He doesn't take it back.

"But Pastor, if I've got all this authority, why does all this junk keep happening to me?"

We have already been through parts of James 1, but right now, let's read verses 2-5. "My brethren, count it all joy when ye fall into divers temptations, knowing this, that the trying of your faith worketh patience. But let patience have her perfect work, that ye may be perfect and entire, wanting nothing. If any of you lack wisdom, let him ask of God, that giveth to all men liberally, and upbraideth not; and it shall be given him."

To "fall" into something means we're not expecting anything like that to happen. If something comes upon us unawares, that is, if we don't know why it came, first we are to rejoice, then ask God to give us wisdom on the matter. We don't rejoice because whatever hit us is fun. Joy and Happy are different. We rejoice because we have just stepped in yet one more Prime Opportunity to prove to the devil and the rest of the world, if they're interested, the all-sufficient grace and power of God. In order for this joy to kick in, we must know that the trial is of our faith, not of us personally. If we don't know this, we will never release the Joy that is resident inside us.

Also, we must know that the spiritual force of Patience (the Greek word means "consistency") is put to work when our faith is put to the test. We decide how much of our patience we are going to release. Know this: we must let patience do its job. If we do, we will end up mature and complete, lacking nothing.

Here is the Bottom Line: God put US in charge of the earth and He will let happen whatever WE will let happen. When we get tired of letting the devil beat us down, we are to take up our spiritual armor, and we are to fight back. When we do, God has guaranteed us success. In order to make it all work for us, God has provided the three most powerful weapons in the universe for you to use.

The first is the Name of Jesus. Acts 3:16 says, "And his name, through faith in his name hath made this man strong, whom ye see and know: yea, the faith which is by him hath given him this perfect soundness in the presence of you all." It is the name of Jesus, and faith in the name of Jesus that made it happen in so many things for the First Century Church. It Still Works Today!!

The second of those unbeatable weapons is the Holy Spirit Himself. Luke 11:9-13 says that our Heavenly Father will surely "... give the Holy Spirit to those that ask him." You can rely on that more than you can rely on getting what you need from your earthly father, no matter how good he may be. Acts 1:8 says that "... ye shall receive power after that the Holy Ghost is come upon you ... " Thank God! We don't have to do anything alone! God has made sure that He is with us in the most intimate way possible and He has covenanted never to leave us.

The third weapon is the Word of God, which is, according to Ephesians 6:17, the "... sword of the spirit ... " which operates out of your spirit, through the name of Jesus, by the power of the Holy Spirit. The Word refers to itself in several ways. Let's look at some of them.

Matthew 4:4 — "Man shall not live by bread alone but by every word that proceedeth out of the mouth of God." The Word is more important than food—live by it!!

Mark 4:14 — "The sower soweth the word." We must plant the Word in the soil of our heart as if it were a seed. No seed can grow unless it is planted.

Luke 10:38-43 — "But one thing is needful, and Mary hath chosen that good part, which shall not be taken from her." The "good part" that Mary chose was to "sit at Jesus' feet and hear His word." The Word is the only thing necessary. If a choice must be made between the Word and something else, choose the "good part".

John 1:1, 14 — "In the beginning was the Word and the Word was with God, and the Word was God. And the Word was made flesh and dwelt among us (and we beheld his glory, the glory as of the only begotten of the father) full of grace and truth." The Word is Jesus is the Word. Jesus is the Word is Jesus. To approach one is to approach the other.

John 17:17 — "Thy word is truth." There is nothing higher and there is no more final Bottom Line.

Romans 10:8 — "But what saith it? The word is nigh thee, even in thy mouth, and in thy heart: that is, the word of faith, which we preach." We must put the Word in our mouth, and keep it there, and it will get into our heart. Our mouth is the key.

Romans 10:17 — "So then, faith cometh by hearing, and hearing by the Word of God." The more we hear the Word (and speaking the Word is the easiest way to "hear" it), the more faith it can create in us. There is a simple one-to-one correlation.

1 John 2:5 — "But whoso keepeth his word, in him verily is the love of God perfected: hereby know we that we are in him." Keeping the Word (in other words, doing the Word) brings the love of God to maturity in us.

Revelation 12:11 — "And they overcame him by the blood of the Lamb and by the word of their testimony, and they loved not their lives unto the death." Use the Word to overcome the devil.

The difference between a millionaire and the rest of us, is not the number of dollars in his pocket, it is the way he thinks!

The difference between an overcomer and a defeated Christian is not in their experiences; it is in the way they think. We all think according to the way we have been taught. If we have been taught something that is in error, no matter how well intentioned, our ability to walk in victory is at serious risk.

Church, our Pastors and other teachers are not responsible for our walk in God. Our parents are not responsible for our walk in God. Our Pastors, teachers and parents are responsible to do the very best they can to get it as close to right as possible, but in the final analysis, we, and we alone, are responsible for our walk in God. The Father believes in us, and He needs for us to lead our section of the Body of Christ to victory. We must turn on our brain. The one God gave us is a good one. We cannot allow ourselves the luxury of swallowing wholesale what somebody teaches us, even if we like the way they teach. It does not matter who it may be—me or anyone else—don't be afraid to ask questions, and don't be afraid to go the Bible to find the answers. What the world needs now is not an updated Phariseeism, but REAL answers, for REAL people, living in the REAL world.

So, if you don't know what else to do, or where else to start, grab yourself by the ear, drag yourself in front of your Bible, and GET REAL and GET FREE!

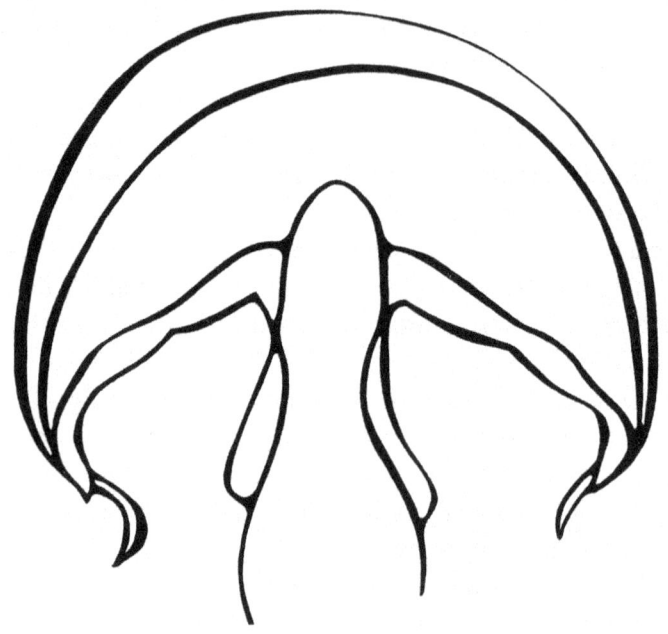

Grateful Acknowledgements

Most deeply and most profoundly, I want to thank my wife, Delonn for the years of strength and encouragement she has invested in me in the writing of this book. She has been a major force in removing many of my rough edges and keeping me focused on what is truly important, rather than ranting or riding hobby horses. Her value to me is indeed, "far above rubies."

I also want to thank my children, Shawn and Talitha, and their mates who have also given unselfishly of their time in helping with the editing processes. I love their insights, and I am ridiculously proud of them, in every way.

My two sisters, Rosannah and Sharon, have each contributed to the editing of this book. The passion for the English language and the passion for the Word of God in my sisters have been invaluable to me in making my heart understandable and clear.

My hearfelt graditude goes to-

Elektra Hendrickson for the art work interspersed throughout this book. We are so priviledged to know her work and talent—she can be reached at TheStarsAreForYou@gmail.com.

Tammy Lind for her proofreading and editing skills in fine tuning this original manuscript. You can't take the country out of the boy, but she was certainly able to polish things up and make them presentable.

Jared Green for his layout and cover design work, for taking our mess of Word docs and emails and turning them into something wonderful. Jared can be contacted for graphic design work at www.redjarcreative.com.

A special thank you to Alan & Gay Rickertsen. Without their love, support & encouragement through the years this book would not be possible. Thank you both for asking the hard questions.

Finally, dear reader, I want to thank you. The hunger in your heart for answers that don't require an advanced degree in Theological Gymnastics is responsible for the draw placed on my heart by the Holy Spirit, which produced this book. God loves to answer questions in honest hearts. Stay hungry. Don't stop asking questions. In God's Grand Scheme Of Things, you are more important than you know.

www.ingramcontent.com/pod-product-compliance
Lightning Source LLC
Chambersburg PA
CBHW071708040426
42446CB00011B/1968